TRUTH AND FEAR

BREAKING FREE FROM RELIGIOUS FUNDAMENTALISM

DANIEL R. KRAUSE

Special thanks to my wife, Diane Louise Krause, my best friend, and cheerleader; a "Jersey Girl," not a "Meeting girl," for her support and input.

To Bud, Robert H. Krause, my friend, mentor and uncle, for his love, patience and endurance in shining light on a path forward out of darkness.

To a few people who I grew up with in the Meeting, who shall not be named.
And to a few people who gave me critical feedback on earlier versions of this book.

You all know who you are.
Thanks very much!

ISBN 979-8-9924219-0-3

Cover design by James, GoOnWrite.com

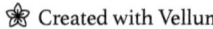 Created with Vellum

PREFACE

In Edward Abbey's essay, *Writer's Credo*[1] he writes (p. 161) "it is my belief that the writer, the free-lance author, should be and must be a critic of the society in which he lives." Why? "To make the world better" he says, quoting Samuel Johnson, "to tell my story" (p. 187). This book represents part of my story. It's also a critique of people who not only hold strong beliefs in a superior being, but in doing so, feel called by their god and empowered to force their beliefs on other people.

This book is for people who believe truth exists, reality, not as they desire to subjectively see it, but as best they can objectively discern it. For whom an uncomfortable truth is preferred over a comfortable lie. For people who agree that while truth may not be immediately evident, the quest to uncover or discover truth, as best they can, is a valid use of their time and effort. And for people who are willing to ask themselves: How do I know, what I think I know, is true?

There are many people who seek to accumulate money, power or both, by undermining people's efforts to discern the truth. The daily news is full of reports of these dishonest people's efforts. Politicians, religious figures, and others who seek to exploit people's feelings, biases and hopes by making false promises that do not survive objective analysis. These include power-hungry zealots, charismatics, fanatics, fundamentalists, and money-hungry swindlers. This book is written to provide an antidote to these people and their dishonesty.

The topics in this book represent ideas human beings have contemplated for millennia. There may be people who suggest that writing this book was a colossal waste of my time; that religion is a topic of absolutes not worth arguing about. For me, this book, yes, took and is taking time away from my limited time alive on this planet, but it also served as a catharsis; a way for me to put some perspective on times during my life, especially my childhood, where time was indeed wasted thinking about and dwelling on topics for which there are no absolute answers, proclaiming to know the unknowable. It also, if I may be so bold, affords me the opportunity to attempt to influence readers' ways of thinking about truth and how to discern it.

However, I do wonder, as I look back over many years, how my religious belief held strong for so long. In my defense, I emphasize the social and parental environment in which I grew up. Children tend to believe what their parents believe, at least until they perceive they've been deceived. And if the beliefs taught dogmatically by one's parents are presented unapologetically and without doubt as true, the resulting beliefs may have long-lasting effects and unintended, even unwelcome consequences.

Although I was raised in an environment with dogmatic religious beliefs, these beliefs weren't something I brought up in everyday conversations once I became an adult and ventured into a wider world. But I remember being astonished, when in my thirties I met somebody who said: "my parents never mentioned a god, God, or gods, so it never crossed my mind to think about it much." I had to sit down to ponder that statement. I was shocked. To not have a question about the existence of God, or gods, was simply not possible for me. In fact, it was *the* primary question of my life! "How could you not think about it?"... I asked. The answer was a simple shrug of shoulders... "that question wasn't important in my household; we never talked about it. As I grew up, I asked my parents if I could go to church, and they said 'sure, go ahead.' But there was never any indication that doing so would be a mistake. It was just learning about the world." – This example is the polar opposite of my experience.

IN READING this book, please note: I use the term "fundamentalist" to describe the social group in which I grew up. Although academic experts have yet to reach consensus as to the definition of the term and who it applies to, I use "fundamentalist" to describe people who read their religious texts literally. In this book I'm primarily referring to Christians and their Bible, as the divinely inspired, unerring word of their God. There are no gray areas from a fundamentalist's view; either you're a believer or not. Either you are "saved" or not. You are bound either for heaven or hell.

Fundamentalist believers with whom I'm familiar believe they hold the absolute truth; just ask them! The earth is not their home. They are travelers here on earth with no yearning to improve it. – I also use the term "fanatic" nearly interchangeably with "fundamentalist." However, I view a "fanatic" as somebody who is overzealous. In my experience, most fundamentalists are fanatics. Fanatical fundamentalists tend to talk in absolutes. They are right. Anybody who disagrees with them is wrong. From my encounters, the belief-characteristics of fanatics appear to be undifferentiated across the various religions, whether they be Christians, Mormons, Jehovah's Witnesses, Scientologists or something else.

A FEW NOTES on my use of abbreviations, primarily KJV, J.N.D., and LFHB. KJV is the King James Version, which is the version of the Bible we primarily used in Meeting, or "the Meeting," our place of worship. J.N.D. is John Nelson Darby, a revered evangelist who was a prominent figure at the inception of "the Meeting," a.k.a., Plymouth Brethren, in the mid-1800s, and according to some people's writings and recollections, one of its founders. J.N.D. is credited with recovering "lost truths" such as the rapture. He was a lawyer and scholar who consulted original texts to write a J.N.D. version of the Bible, thought by some believers to be a more accurate translation than the KJV. People in the Meeting often consult J.N.D.'s version of the Bible when there is a doctrinal question not resolved in the KJV.

LFHB stands for *A Few Hymns and Some Spiritual Songs, Selected 1856, For the Little Flock,*[2] or the "Little Flock Hymn Book," as we called it, which was and is the hymn book used in the Meeting, except for Sunday night Gospel Meeting where we used the *Echoes of Grace Hymn Book.*[3]

Finally, many names of people who appear in this book have been changed to preserve their anonymity.

1

FAMILY

I grew up in the 1960s and 70s. I was an outcast, at least I felt that way, living on the fringes of society. Not economically, for my father had a decent job at a large industrial company. No, I was a social outcast. My father and mother were "members of the body of Christ" in a group of fundamentalist Christians who believed they were saved from hell by the suffering and shed-blood of Christ. The group met at a place we called "the Meeting." – "Whosoever believeth in Him should not perish, but have everlasting life." My parents fervently believed that passage from John 3:16 (KJV), and that secured their futures for eternity.

We lived in the southern, rolling hills of New York state, about five miles west of Endicott, birthplace of IBM, Big Blue. At its local peak, IBM employed over 10,000 people in the area, including my father. But the company has since largely abandoned the place. All that remains are millions of square feet of buildings and grounds, with "International Business Machines" carved in drooping stone. The town has begun to tear those buildings down. Big business graveyard. I think the founder of IBM, Thomas J. Watson, would spin in his grave if he saw the place now. But that's just my opinion.

Our home was situated in a neighborhood of houses built on sub-divided half-acre parcels of the old Pearsall farm. We picked strawberries at nearby farms and paid by the quart. The area isn't far, just a three-to-four hour bicycle ride in my experience, from Ithaca, where Concord grapes and apples grew in abundance. Locally, The Cider Mill served apple cider and donuts. You could watch them process the apples, filling one-gallon glass jugs with the brown, sweet liquid. To me, the place smelled heavenly.

As soon as I was old enough, I made money mowing lawns, selling seeds and greeting cards door-to-door, and delivering the local newspaper on foot and bike. I soon found that selling door-to-door didn't play to my strengths, but I did enjoy delivering newspapers. Most people appeared to enjoy receiving their newspaper via a local kid, and I was often received by a quick, cheerful greeting. But I also had to collect payment for these deliveries which could be time-consuming and frustrating.

There were about twenty kids in the neighborhood, and by some estimates, fifty cats, none of which were ours. In the summer, we played kickball and football, rode our bicycles, built tree forts, and fished and frolicked in the local creek. In the winter, we ice skated, played hockey, went sledding and tobogganing, and had snowball fights.

But it wasn't all fun and games. Three kids died in a short period of time. Karen, five years old, had a heart problem. She would run with us for a few minutes until her cherubic face turned blue. Then she would squat with a smile on her face and watch the rest of us play. I was pretty young, but remember that she left to have a heart operation from which she didn't return. A boy next door, Jimmy Fish, drowned in the local creek when it was in flood stage; he was about eleven. Riding his bicycle, he used to peruse the sides of the roads near our house, looking for half-smoked cigarettes, which he would light up with a big smile. Ricky E., just down the street, hanged himself in his family's garage. He had gone to Sunday School with us a few times. Mom thought he was saved. But his father was an alcoholic and didn't pay much attention to him. A local rumor was that he never took another drink after Ricky died.

I have three siblings; I am the oldest, followed by my brother Dwight, and sisters Silvie and Sharon. Our father, Charles, grew up in the midwestern USA, on the outskirts of Detroit. He attended Meeting with his parents in Detroit, along with his brother Robert, who Dad nicknamed Bud. Their parents, Harold and Edna, were descendants of Swiss-German and Swedish immigrants, respectively, who emigrated to the USA in the mid-1800s. Harold graduated from Drake University, and worked for one of the tire manu-facturers as a chemist. Until he died, in his nineties, I never saw him wear any other footwear than wingtip shoes; polished ones for going to Meeting, and paint-speckled wingtips for doing odd jobs around our house or mowing the lawn. He stood ramrod straight until the day he died, and I think his posture was an outward manifestation of his religious fanaticism, that of "bringing into captivity every thought to the obedience of Christ" (II Corinthians 10:5, KJV).

Bud's and Dad's mother, Edna, was a home-maker, attended college in Iowa, and graduated, as best I can tell, with a degree in home economics. She was one of the Larson sisters, daughters of Swedish immigrants. Their father, Albert, was a laboring brother in the Meeting, meaning that he travelled from Meeting to Meeting, preaching and ministering to the needs of the saints, a term used to describe people in the Meeting, for which he received their voluntary financial support. Edna died in her early fifties of diabetes when I was quite young. My only memory of her is me sitting next to her at the piano while she played and sang hymns.

Our mother, Marilyn, was born in the front room of a large farmhouse outside of Leamington, Ontario, Canada. Her mother, Velma, was a hard-working woman with Irish roots, who raised five kids on an economic shoestring. She never drove a car, and I remember walking downtown in Leamington, where she seemed to know everybody and everybody knew her. Mom's father, Garnet, had the opportunity to farm for a living, but chose instead to start a marginally successful plumbing and heating company. He rarely smiled, seemed eternally unhappy about the course of USA politics, and from my limited observations, treated Velma poorly. He had fairly enormous ears, which someone in the family dubbed "Garnet Beauties," so-named after a local variety of peach. He had a reasonably well-concealed cigarette addiction; never smoked in the house or in view of his grandchildren, but the clingy, rancid smell was difficult to conceal. Mom's ancestors reportedly emigrated to eastern Canada from Scotland and Ireland in the 1600s. She attended Meeting in southern Ontario with her family, at Chatham, although her father was not a regular attendee. A weekly Bible-reading Meeting was held in the front room of her parents' Leamington home. She met my father at Meeting.

Leamington had a large Heinz factory in town when I was a kid, and I remember farmers driving into town on their tractors, pulling wagons piled high with tomatoes. The town smelled of tomatoes and ketchup. The kids in the neighborhood used to have tomato wars in the fields with the remnants of the tomato crop. My brother and I would come in for our evening bath plastered in tomato soup. Neighboring farms grew peaches, cherries, apples and tobacco. I worked several summers, picking fruit in the orchards, and making the trip to the big farm-market in Windsor, early Saturday mornings, to sell the crop. Those summers of my childhood shine bright.

THE MEETING IS the backdrop on the life-stage on both sides of our family. We belonged to the Vestal, NY Meeting, but also attended Meetings in Detroit, MI, and Athens, Enola, Harveyville, and Scranton, PA. We also attended large, annual Bible Conferences in Illinois, Quebec, Ohio, and Pennsylvania.

The social relationships within the Meeting represent a common thread that explains, from generation to generation, many marriages within the Meeting. The chance that my parents would have otherwise met if not in the Meeting is nearly zero. This fact leads to the obvious conclusion: without the Meeting, my siblings and I would not exist.

2

CLOSE CALLS

S igns painted on streets at busy intersections in London, England implore visitors to "look right" because so many look left from habit, and not looking right nearly gets them run over. Stepping off the curb without looking; forgetting to put the drain plug in the bottom of a boat; moving a car's shifter into neutral hoping to coast forward a few feet while forgetting that without the key turned on the steering wheel is locked and the brakes don't work – some close calls are more serious than others. Many can be explained by youthful enthusiasm, lack of experience, or both. Some can be forgiven because they are a result of ignorance or stupidity. Some stick with you; others are forgotten.

One of my mother's close calls, recalled vividly by me because I feared I might have lost her, was when she attempted to move a car with which she was unfamiliar. The car was blocking her vehicle, and when she stepped on the clutch and slid the shifter into neutral, the steering wheel locked and the car plummeted a couple hundred feet down a hillside, ramming head-on into a tree. I found out about it only the next morning, when she appeared at Meeting, our family place of worship, with broken glasses, a black eye and swollen cheekbones. I ached for her! I thought about how the hill was steep and long and how things could have been much worse. In a panic, she'd finally managed to stomp on the emergency brake, but by then the damage was done. My parents laughed it off, saying "the Lord takes care of His own." I wasn't so sure. If so, why hadn't he warned her?

My mom's close call was based on ignorance. She thought she could gently coast the car out of the way, but didn't understand how the new car functioned. She appeared to forget about her close call because I don't recall her ever mentioning it again.

THE CLOSE CALL I remember most vividly, and recall again from time to time, is etched indelibly in my mind because of what a difference an inch or two can make. In my case, I was fortunate; the inches were in my favor. Had they gone the other way, I could have been seriously injured, even killed.

Our family spent many happy days of my childhood visiting various members of my mother's family in southern Ontario. While growing up, I had the benefit of experiencing her interactions with her three sisters, her brother, their spouses and her parents – my aunts, uncles and grandparents. Aunt Elaine and Uncle Jerry purchased a small farm when I was about ten, and my grandparents also lived on a farm. Elaine and Jerry were part-time farmers, raising kids, working regular jobs and tending fourteen acres they planted in apples, peaches and pears. I was enamored of the farm. The neighboring farms grew tobacco, various fruits and tomatoes. The earth was dark brown and fertile and I reveled in the sights, sounds and smells of farm life. And I was hugely fascinated by Uncle Jerry's old, gray Ford tractor.

During one of our post-Christmas visits, Jerry drove the old tractor out to the back of their fourteen acres, dragging a once-was Christmas tree. I went with him, sitting up on the fender of the old Ford. We hooked a chain around the tree's trunk and pulled it down the snowy lane to a compost pile of sorts. The snow was easily a foot deep, perhaps deeper as it was up to my knees. Inside the house, a fire was crackling in the wood stove and hot chocolate awaited our return. At the compost pile, we dropped the tree, pushed it up on a pile of similar debris and left it there for spring. For some reason, and although he's still alive I won't be asking him, my uncle jumped back on the tractor and took off without me. I think he was trying to have a bit of fun. He knew how much I loved that tractor. He had let me drive it a couple of times, carefully supervised. But care went out the window that day. He threw the tractor into gear and headed for the barn. I ran after him through the deep snow. The problem was that the chain was still lying deep in the snow, dragged behind the tractor.

Excited at being left behind, I was unaware of the chain's presence or position. Turns out it was right between my legs. I heard it, hissing through the foot-deep snow. Soon after, I tripped and fell. Almost simultaneously I experienced the sensation of falling, hearing the chain being pulled through the snow inches beneath my head, and feeling, or at least hearing, a ripping sound somewhere down below. I stood up to see the chain and its evil hook following the tractor, leaving me behind. I looked down to see the crotch of my pants tattered and gone! So were my underwear. My privates hung in the cold, dark January air, with a minor scratch but thankfully intact.

I don't remember many specific details immediately afterward. Uncle Jerry arrived back at the barn unaware of the event. Next thing I remember, I was warming up in the main bathroom of the house, and my father, ashen-faced, stepped in to ask if everything was all right. I noted that there was a slight scrape on my penis, but that everything else was quite intact. My father laughed, a bit giddily I thought, and said "thank the Lord." He, I assume like me, had thoughts running through his mind about what might have happened if that hook had been an open hook versus a closed one that catches a chain link, or if the hook had been a bit higher in the snow.

To this day, when I think about this close call, I shudder at the implications. The hook might have dismembered me, ripped my chin off or otherwise ruined me. At the time, Uncle Jerry was understandably upset, embarrassed and having a hard time forgiving himself. It's one of those stories that make most owners of male genitalia slap their knees together, take a long swig from an open bottle, or grab an unopened one. This close call, indelibly etched in my brain, is often followed by contemplations of life in general, its propensities, its probabilities, and our general lack of fore-sight and control.

I was just a kid when this accident occurred, roughly ten years old. My lack of experience, youthful enthusiasm for the tractor and life on the farm, and my uncle's oversight could have inalterably changed my life forever. – My father thanked the Lord I had been spared from serious injury. Me? I was happy with my hot chocolate, warm pajamas, and an esteemed spot by the wood stove.

But the implications of that close-call would have time to marinate in my brain, which would put the event into perspective and eventually be one of many catalysts leading to questions that had uncomfortable answers. Why did this happen to me? Why is there pain and suffering in the world? Why does God allow bad things to happen? Does He know? Does He care? Many of these unanswered questions were the result of me being the target of forced religious indoctrination from the womb in what could arguably be called a fundamentalist Christian cult, where belief was carefully cultivated, questions discouraged, and skepticism was sin.

3

GROWING UP IN "THE MEETING"

My parents' primary purpose in life was to "live for Him," God, in all respects, and to raise their children in the "nurture and admonition of the Lord" (Ephesians 6:4, KJV). We attended "the Meeting," or Meeting. Years later, I came to understand that, for tax purposes, the government called us Plymouth Brethren. But we didn't call ourselves that. We were an exclusive group of Christians to whom the truth had been revealed. "For where two or three are gathered together in my name, there am I in the midst of them," said Jesus, according to the Bible, Matthew 18:20, (KJV). We believed it and acted accordingly.

Sunday morning, or "The Lord's Day" as we called it, consisted of Sunday School at 10am, then Breaking of Bread at 11am, where we believed the Holy Spirit was orchestrating the proceedings. Sunday evenings we attended Gospel. Wednesday and Friday evenings were, respectively, Prayer Meeting and Reading Meeting. There was no formally designated preacher, pastor or priest, only men, or Brothers, as they referred to each other, who were led by the Holy

Spirit to participate. If a traveling or so-called laboring brother was in town, special Meetings were held on alternate nights. Musical instruments were not part of the proceedings; only human voices raised in songs of praise.

My religious indoctrination was pervasive – and made so deliberately by my parents, who feared that if heavenly thoughts weren't continuously put in front of us, the devil would creep in much like cold creeps into a house during a windy, winter storm. If the heat goes out during the storm, the house begins to cool almost immediately, and if Jesus Christ wasn't put in front of us continuously, the devil would creep in and diminish the joy that only Jesus could provide. Thus, my father read the Bible to my brother and me over breakfast every morning before school. He gave thanks before every meal. In the evenings, we read the Bible and prayed together, on our knees, as a family.

So, I describe myself as a social outcast, that is in relation to people in the outside world, outside of the Meeting. One line of a song we sang was: "We're pilgrims in the wilderness; Our dwelling is a camp" (#231, LFHB).[1] For us, camp meant no TV, no radio and minimal interaction with non-believers.

The Brethren thought of themselves as more advanced, more biblically correct than anybody else, with exclusively-held truth. We weren't allowed to join any non-Meeting group. Doing so was entering into an unequal yoke with unbelievers; strictly forbidden (II Corinthians 6:14, KJV). For me and my siblings, that meant no joining the Boy or Girl Scouts, and no involvement in school sports or other extra-curricular activities. For my father, it meant not purchasing stock, which was available to him at a discount, in the company where he worked. And what I later considered to be one of his most ludicrous convictions, not becoming a member of the local credit union. Of course, marriages outside the Meeting were highly discouraged. Even self-described Christians such as Catholics or Baptists were out of bounds for marriage or social relationships. We held the truth; they did not. So, our social circle was almost completely composed of people who belonged to the Meeting.

Soon after birth, I was circumcised. Obviously I was too young to remember it, but when I was older I heard my father discuss circumcision with his Meeting brethren. They agreed that circumcision was painful, but symbolically represented our chosen Christian pathway. Eschewing the pleasures of the world in our lives came with pain, a cutting off of worldly pleasures – being separate from the world. But our reward was awaiting us in heaven. As a young child I was baptized by Harry Hayhoe, a prominent, revered laboring brother in the Meeting. Again, I was too young to remember it, but this procedure was an important indicator of my parents' dedication of me to Christ.

Sex was a forbidden topic in our household. Sex outside of marriage was sin. Sex before marriage was sin. Even thinking about the opposite sex in lustful ways was sin. I remember a brother in the Denver Meeting who had two teenage sons. According to them, their dad drove out of their way to go to Meeting so as to avoid passing by a bill-board with a picture of a half-naked woman. And although I never was able to independently verify it beyond hearing the same report from several people, one brother in the Meeting in New Jersey had such a spiritual exercise about a doctor seeing his wife's private parts that he delivered their baby himself in the privacy of their own home.

The old joke about Christians not having sex while standing up because it might lead to dancing is funny because it's true. Dancing was strictly forbidden because it was almost-sex. Besides, we didn't listen to worldly music, and dancing to songs like "Jesus loves me; this I know" doesn't work very well. Music, for us, was primarily to praise God. – When I was about ten, my father bought a new car, used but new to us, and it came with a built-in radio. I was excited! But my excitement was short-lived when about one week after the purchase the radio disappeared and ensconced in its place sat a carefully painted gray board.

As a result of our adopted rules for living, I had few cultural references with the outside world, although I did attend public school. There I was ridiculed because I was "weird" and didn't participate in any extracurricular activities: no dances, no sports or social engagements; they weren't allowed. – My neighborhood peers knew some of what went on inside our home. They knew we didn't celebrate Easter, Halloween or Christmas. These were worldly holidays, according to my parents, and things of the world were shunned. We never had a Christmas tree. Halloween was "of the devil." And we celebrated Jesus' triumph over death every Sunday, or The Lord's Day; so Easter was redundant.

Our neighbors also knew we didn't have a TV or a radio. One of my father's Meeting peers called the big, unwieldy rooftop TV antennas prevalent in those days the "devil's tail;" there wouldn't be one on our house. Worldly events and news were generally unknown to us, unless one of the neighbors knocked on the door to inform us, as they did when Robert F. Kennedy was shot. Clearly my father must have heard of world events at work, but we were *in* the world, not *of* it. However, we did sometimes receive the local newspaper during the week, delivered to our front porch, but not the Sunday edition.

The Meeting was exclusively centered on worshipping God the Father, and his Son, the Lord, Jesus Christ. God, who we believed had created the universe, had created Adam first, made Eve of Adam's rib and made her subservient. This was the natural order of things and you didn't question the order God had imposed on the universe. So, women were not allowed to speak during Meeting. They covered their heads and kept silent. Only once in twenty years did I hear a woman speak up in Meeting; she had come in off the street and clearly didn't know her place.

Married women were to be subservient to their husbands (Genesis 3:16, KJV). When my father gave thanks for the food at the beginning of the meal, Mom covered her head with her hand. A woman's glory was her hair; it needed to be covered (I Corinthians 11:15, KJV). I knew if Mom was concerned about something in her life because she would work around the house with a kerchief on her head. She was praying.

The women in the Meeting, including Mom and my sisters, did not wear men's clothing, at least the ones who were trying to please God. Skirts and dresses were the only permissible dress; their hair was worn long. In a few exceptions pants might be allowed, but only if worn under a dress. Years after I grew up, I began to see my mother in culottes; this was a sign, to me, of a less legal, slightly more permissive environment.

My mother was Canadian, and missed her home and her sisters, brother and parents. She was kind and loved people and animals, but was absolutely terrified of snakes. In Genesis 3:15 (KJV), God says to the serpent: "I will put enmity between thee and the woman, and between thy seed and her seed; it shall bruise thy head, and thou shalt bruise his heel." However you interpret that biblical passage, I do know that snakes bruised the heel of my mother's mind. She couldn't even look at a caricature of a snake let alone a picture, without doing a sharp intake of breath, and putting her hand over her heart.

Mom was the fun-lover in the family; laughter almost always originated from her. She never lost the ability or the inclination to play. We played games for family entertainment, but only those that didn't include dice or playing cards. These were manifestations of gambling; not allowed. But we played Rook, Monopoly, Crokinole, and Chess, among others. – Today, I attribute the humanity and kindness I often feel toward my fellow humans to my mother. She was the one who went to my father and pleaded for leniency, to see things our way. At the same time, she was a fervent believer in Christ, and often sat at the table after breakfast, with a kerchief covering her hair, reading her Bible.

Mom never held a job while I was growing up, even though she wanted one. She had held a job in sales in a department store in Detroit after she married my father and during the time he was in Korea. He had been drafted, registered as a conscientious objector, and as such had not been required to touch a gun. But he served two years in a medical tent, aiding the wounded. He rarely talked about it. My parents had married before Dad shipped off to Korea, and it was considered appropriate that Mom work while he was off at war. After he returned, she never worked in a paid job outside the house. For her, keeping the house, looking after four kids and attending to social activities with Meeting-folk filled her days.

Mom was an accomplished cook. Lord's Day lunches

were typically roasted beef, mashed potatoes, gravy, cooked vegetables, the rest of the bread from that morning's Breaking of Bread, and a beautiful pie, lemon, cherry, pecan or apple. We often had company, either visitors from other Meetings or some of the locals. Mom loved to cook and loved to have company.

THERE WERE several families in our local Meeting and we often socialized together. Mr. R. worked for a local municipality; Mr. D. was a chemist at IBM; Mr. P. was a machinist at IBM; Mr. L. was retired from a local shoe manufacturer; Mr. K. was retired; Mr. C., like my father, worked for IBM. Mr. I., or Uncle Jim as I called him, was self-employed. Most of the women, who were the Mrs. part of the equation, were homemakers.

There were other people in the Meeting, singles. These I would describe mostly as social outcasts of one sort or another, not readily fitting in to the family environment of the Meeting. If you were in the Meeting, you were either born into it, married into it, or, with few exceptions a social misfit.

I was born into the Meeting. So, also was my father, his father, his grandfather, his great-grandfather, and his great-great grandfather, going back to western Switzerland, when in the 1850s, my great-great-great grandfather moved with his wife and family to St. Louis, Missouri. Johan August Teodore Krause, or J.A.T. as our family calls him, had met John Nelson Darby, the pre-eminent evangelist in the Meeting, during one of Darby's visits to western Switzerland. According to my grandfather Harold, my dad's father, J.A.T. had become convicted of his status as a sinner and had accepted Jesus Christ as his personal Savior.

John Nelson Darby was, and still is, revered as one of the primary forefathers and founders of the Meeting. An internet search yields thousands of sources of information on Darby, and a search on Amazon.com yields several hundred more, so I will keep my description short. Born in London in 1800, educated at Trinity College in Dublin, Darby was by some descriptions employed as a young lawyer in London in the early 1820s. Other sources say he never practiced law.[2] Regardless, in his early twenties he began a spiritual quest for the truth. This search led him to being ordained as a deacon in the Church of England.

Descriptions of a young Darby depict a man willing to forego the pleasures of spending a rather sizable inheritance on a comfortable lifestyle in favor of helping the poor. Increasingly unhappy with established religion, including the Church of England, Darby started meeting with like-minded people in Plymouth, England, a group of people who eventually became known as Plymouth Brethren. Darby's focus was on the Bible, which he viewed as *the* Word of God. The Church had, in Darby's view, lost its way and lost its hold on the truth.

Many of Darby's beliefs appear to have been formed during a period when he was recovering from a knee injury suffered while riding a horse. During his convalescence, he reached several significant conclusions: i) that the Bible was the unerring, divine Word of God, ii) that as a believer in Christ he was saved and bound for an eternal life in heaven, iii) that being saved, he already had a place reserved for him in heaven, iv) that Jesus Christ was, at any moment, going to return from heaven to earth to claim his earthly Bride, which was the word Christ used to collectively describe true believers, and v) that the rapture would be followed by the tribulation as described in the biblical books of Isaiah and

Revelations, when God would once again punish sinners with retributory violence.[2]

Darby's gravestone includes the inscription: "Lord let me wait for Thee alone, My life is only this, To serve Thee here on earth unknown, Then share Thy heavenly bliss. J.N.D." Darby made several evangelizing trips to parts of Europe, the USA and Canada. During at least one of those trips he visited western Switzerland where he met my great-great-great grandfather, J.A.T., who with his family was living in La Chaux-de-Fonds.

As far as I know, this meeting of J.A.T. Krause with J.N.D. marks the beginning of religious fundamentalism in my family. J.A.T. was a watch and clock maker, as many in that region were at that time. Today, La Chaux-de-Fonds is home to the International Museum of Horology, or clock making. Family lore includes the story that Darby gave J.A.T a significant amount of money at that time to help move his family to the USA. That move occurred in the early 1850s. – I have among my possessions a grandfather clock, made by J.A.T. and two wooden chests that came over on the boat that departed out of Hamburg, Germany. The family landed in St. Louis, after burying two young children at sea who died of cholera during the voyage.

My family also has J.A.T.'s "Wanderbuch," which is a book of the various apprenticeships he held on his journeyman's way to becoming a watch and clock maker. The internal workings of the grandfather clock he made are amazing to observe, as my grandfather put it. The pendulum weighs approximately 18 pounds and the clock keeps excellent time. It hung as a regulator in a train station in St. Louis, for some time, serving as the local official time keeper back in the early 1900s.

Years ago as a relatively young man, I was asked by my

grandfather Harold, my father's-father, if I would type up some written notes he had assembled on our family history, with a special focus on J.A.T. I was excited at the opportunity to learn something about my family history, but disappointed at the notes my grandfather provided. Unfortunately, they included conjectural speculation about how somebody had asked J.A.T about the status of his soul, and that question served "as an arrow from God's quiver," pricking his conscience, whereupon he turned to the Lord and was saved. According to my grandfather, J.A.T. was also described by some of his acquaintances as a tyrant. This description strikes me as appropriate for a religious fundamentalist and fanatic. Unhappily, I have to say this characteristic seems to have trickled down through several generations to include my own grandfather and father.

4

MEETING RITUALS, TEACHINGS
AND FAILURES

I t's difficult to fully convey how saturated our lives were with fundamentalist Christian beliefs. By age ten, I had sat for several thousand hours of Bible study; that's how I learned to read. Fundamentalist in this case means that we took the Bible literally as the unerring word of God and *the* source of truth. If an idea or fact contradicted the Bible, that idea or fact was in error. I use a capital G, because our God was the only one and true god. All other gods were invalid. In the biblical book of Matthew, chapter 6, verse 19, Jesus extolls his disciples to lay up treasures in heaven by doing good works for Him and God. Like Jesus' disciples, we were either laying up treasure in heaven or we were wasting our time. This lens through which we viewed life was, to us, clear and unfiltered and guided us in our daily activities to do things that pleased God and to always be expecting his return to earth via the rapture.

All around us in the outside world was sin and the products of sin, namely human suffering, pain and life-paths leading to destruction. This view of life is expounded upon in *The Pilgrim's Progress*,[1] if you are unlucky enough to be familiar with that particular piece of Christian fiction. I read this book when I was quite young; it gave me nightmares. Destruction meant eternity in hell unless a person repented of their sins and believed in God. Thus, it was important to immerse ourselves in the Word of God, the Bible.

Academics who study and seek to understand fundamentalism have identified at least nine characteristics of fundamentalist groups.[2] For fundamentalist Christians, these characteristics manifest as:

Ideological:

- Defense of religious traditions: Fundamentalists think their beliefs are under attack and seek to defend them.
- Selective defense of specific aspects of tradition, e.g., women's God-ordained subservience and lack of control over their own bodies.
- Dualism: Good versus evil; e.g., Jesus said "you are either for me, or against me."
- Absolutism: The Bible as the unerring word of God.
- Millennialism: End of times thinking. The rapture.

Organizational:

- Exclusivity: Believers alone hold recovered truth and must defend it from evil.
- Distinct boundaries: Believers are saved; unbelievers are not.
- Authoritarianism: Charismatic leaders, often viewed as god-ordained, rise to lead the pack, but

when these leaders disagree, splits occur as each side claims *the* exclusive right to divine truth.

- Behavioral restrictions: e.g., pertaining to drinking, gambling, sex, dress, authority of elders, social boundaries, etc.

I think the Meeting in which I was raised fully fits these characteristics. We sang hymns wherein we were Christian soldiers, marching to war. We were fighting against the forces of evil, not only Satan, but also other religious entities that did not hold the truth and were thus in Satan's control. Most of these characteristics are divisive and exclusionary, separating Meeting-believers from everybody else.

Missing from the above characteristics is the arrogance exhibited by many fundamentalists that results from believing they are right and everybody else is wrong. This characteristic manifests itself in varying degrees at the individual level, and shows up in people like my father and grandfather. – While the degrees of rigidity and adherence to biblical doctrine varied across members of the Meeting, I think my father is easily classified as one of the more stringent fathers in our local Meeting, unbending in his beliefs and fully resolved in his enforcement of them within our family.

Each week started with Sunday. Sunday was the Lord's Day, a sacred day, period! We were rarely allowed to change into play-clothes on Sunday. No play, this was the Lord's Day. Sunday School was primarily focused on children. We were split into age-based groups, and gathered in various corners of the Meeting room to concentrate on lessons from the Bible. Most of those specific lessons are lost from memory, but mental tapes remain and often play uninvited when I encounter overtly religious people, their symbols, traditions and places of worship.

I've never been much of a morning person, so the droning on of one of the Meeting brothers pontificating about some story in the Bible did little to stimulate my interest, especially during my early teen years. But as a little kid, immersed from the womb in love of the Bible and the Lord, Jesus Christ, it was all I knew. I loved the various songs we sang: "Jesus loves me, this I *know*, for the Bible tells me so." — "Red and yellow, black and white, all are precious in his sight, Jesus loves the little children of the world." — "He sees what we do and he hears what we say, my Lord is watching all the time, time, time."

Biblical parables were also part of the fabric. Adam and Eve, Cain and Abel, Noah's ark and the flood, God telling Abraham to offer his son Isaac upon the alter, David and Goliath, Jonah and the Whale, Moses and forty years of wandering in the desert, the Prodigal Son, Daniel in the lion's den, Job's trials, the parting of the Red Sea, and so on. These stories became references and touch-points that formed the basis of our understanding of the world as it existed before us and how God interacted with humans.

As described so aptly by Richard Dawkins in his 1995 article entitled "Putting Away Childish Things" in the *Skeptical Inquirer*,[3] credulousness is a fundamental characteristic of children. Children tend to believe uncritically because they lack experience. Dawkins says: "If your parents tell you something that is not true, you will believe (it)" (p. 33). — Clearly life holds many dangers. Children learn by doing, and also by listening to influential adults in their lives, whom they have learned to trust. Influential adults in my life were my mother and father, my grandparents, especially my father's father, Harold, the men or so-called Brothers in the Meeting, and to a lesser extent, the Sisters, as the women were called. If Mom told me to be careful around the stove, else I might get burned, I listened. By listening to these influential and trusted adults, I was able, like most kids, to accelerate my learning and succeed in life with minimal suffering.

Dawkins also identifies gullibility, that of susceptibility to being duped, as another characteristic of children. Children tend to believe in the Easter Bunny, the Tooth Fairy, Santa Claus, and the Man in the Moon, especially if adults tell them they exist. Our parents took great care to inform us that these characters did not exist. In contrast, they stated that Jesus had not only existed on this very earth; he had lived and died for *us*, because of *our* sins. Human beings were sinful, and God hated sin. Jesus had been crucified because I was sinful! God could not look upon us sinners because He was revolted by our sins. Therefore, Jesus had willingly and knowingly allowed himself to be crucified on a cross so I could live with Him forever in heaven. My parents, me, my siblings, our relatives and all our Meeting friends believed this in our hearts; we were all saved and going to heaven for eternity.

During Meeting services, women were to be subservient and were not allowed to speak. This approach fulfilled the Apostle Paul's exhortation in I Timothy 2:11 (KJV), "let the woman learn in silence with all subjection." They sat passively, in silence with their heads covered and, mostly, their heads bowed. The Meeting had no minister, rabbi, or priest, and no equivalent. No musical instruments were present; only human voices raised in songs of praise. Each Meeting was run by the Brothers, the men, who were led by the Holy Ghost to stand up and pray, or to suggest a song, or to read a passage from the Bible. The presence of the Holy Ghost was especially felt during the Breaking of Bread. This hour-long Meeting formally scheduled from 11 a.m. to noon on Lord's Day sometimes went on longer because it was preeminently important.

The Breaking of Bread represented Christ's body broken for us. The passing of the cup of wine, represented his shed-blood. A Brother, incited or inspired by the Holy Ghost, would solemnly rise and approach the table that held the wine and unbroken loaf of bread, which was set in the midst of the fifty or so people attending. He would offer up an earnest prayer before breaking the loaf and passing it around to people who were approved to break bread. This loaf of bread represented the body of Christ, broken on the cross for our sins. These prayers were often filled with agony and solemn, vicarious imaginings of the sufferings of Christ.

By the time I was ten, my father was a seasoned expert in this ritual. His prayers, often lasting ten minutes or more, were filled with vivid imaginings of Christ's sufferings, of the humiliation of being forced to drag his cross up the hill to Golgotha, and the pain and horror of being nailed to a cross, which was placed between two thieves who were also suffering their own crucifixions. Further, having the cross lifted and dropped upright into a hole in the ground, while being nailed to it, must have caused great pain from the nails in Jesus' hands and feet.

But this man-caused suffering was nothing in comparison to the pain and suffering God inflicted on Jesus because of our sins. Untold suffering and agony! Great drops of sweat falling to the ground. Agony and depths of despair unfathomable to humans. Ultimately, Jesus called out "Eloi,

Eloi, lama sabacthani" – "My God, My God, why hast though forsaken me?" Then the final insult, a soldier with a spear pierced his side, and "forthwith came there out blood and water" (John 19:34, KJV). The Brothers who broke bread, my father among them, considered this ritual to be a very solemn privilege, their voices often breaking, tears streaming down their faces as they recounted these events in prayer form. After the bread, came the wine, which represented Christ's shed-blood. Often, in this prayer, there was a recounting of the miracle of Jesus rising from the dead. He had conquered death and the grave. His victory was ours! We only had to believe in Him and we would go to heaven forever.

On Lord's Day afternoons we often invited people who had attended the Breaking of Bread to come home with us for a formal lunch. Afterward, we engaged in Christian fellowship, which often included listening to reel-to-reel tape recordings of Meetings from Bible conferences, where some of the best and brightest minds in the Meeting communed with each other and the Holy Ghost over the Word of God.

Gospel Meeting occurred every Sunday evening. One of the Meeting Brothers, or a traveling Brother, would preach for one hour even if everyone in the room was presumed to be saved, because somebody might walk in off the street. The content of these preachings was either delivered in the form of pleading or one of hell-fire and damnation. We often began with a song from the *Echoes of Grace – Hymn Book*.[4]

One of the songs I remember is:

"What can wash away my sins?

Nothing but the blood of Jesus!
What can make me whole again?
Nothing but the blood of Jesus!

Oh, precious is the flow,
That makes me white as snow;
No other fount I know,
Nothing but the blood of Jesus!" [4]

Singing this song with, say, fifty people was just okay. But when we attended a Bible Conference with 1,000 or more people present, singing this song with the throng made me think "this is what heaven must be like;" it was spine tingling and wonderful.

Another song we often sang included the lines:

"Christ is the Saviour of sinners,
Christ is the Saviour for me;
Long I was chained in sin's darkness,
Now by His grace I am free

Saviour of sinners,
Savior of sinners like me,
Shedding his blood for my ransom,
This is the Saviour for me." [4]

After the song, the Brother would preach. Sometimes the message was one of pleading, or imploring unsaved sinners to accept Christ as their personal Saviour. Doing so would save a person from eternal suffering in hell. This message contrasted markedly, both in content and delivery, with the hell-fire sermons. Here, the emphasis was on the nature of hell, the terribleness of sin, how unworthy and vile we were as unrepentant sinners, and for the unsaved, an eternity spent weeping, wailing and gnashing of teeth in a place where the worm dieth not and the fire is not quenched (Mark 9:48, KJV). If the Brother was charismatic and glib with his words and turn of phrase, and fairly demonstrative, he might work himself into a moderate frenzy about how awful it was to be spending even one more second of our lives as unbelieving, unsaved sinners. He then typically closed his sermon with another song and a prayer. – So, Sundays were lo-o-ong days. I was always happy for Mondays. For me, Sundays were too much religion and not enough of almost anything else.

Yes, non-believers were destined for hell. When I was about ten, I remember my father seeing a group of young people a few years older than me, with dreadlocks and tie-dyed shirts. He described them as "poor heathens." He pitied them. I believe he also looked down on them, seeing them through the eyes of his God as unclean, unrepentant hedonists, bound for hell and suffering for all eternity. Yet there was room in God's house if they would only believe in Him! And that led to my father's habit of handing out gospel tracts wherever we went. He left gospel tracts with tips at restaurants, placed them inside envelopes with his bill payments and handed them to anybody who would take them. He was saved, most people were sinners on the road to hell, and he was doing his part to save them from this fate.

He didn't just hand out gospel tracts. He started the Christian Book Center, CBC for short. It was a sole proprietorship, strictly non-profit and located in the basement of the Meeting. There in a glassed-in case and an assortment of shelves, racks, and a table, he sold Bibles, religious books, and gospel tracts, most of which originated from Bible Truth Publishers in Oak Park, Illinois.

I remember throwing a frisbee or playing catch with my father only a few times in my life, but I do remember our yearly, lonely visits during off-hours to the Meeting-room CBC, doing inventory for year-end reporting. We counted tracts, blew dust off the inventory, and shined the glass. This was the Lord's work. Getting access to quality written works wasn't as easy in those days as it is today, and my father only stocked doctrinally sound works.

The idea of dispensationalism was included in our beliefs. Attributed to J. N. Darby, dispensationalism proposes that history is split into different time periods, or dispensations, where God treats humanity in different ways. The sixth dispensation, the time period during which we were (and are) living, is where Jesus comes back to earth to rapture believers. The idea of the rapture, along with eternal life from believing in Jesus, came primarily from Darby as "recovered truth;" truth that had been lost by the various churches over hundreds of years.

Certainty regarding the truth was of primary importance to my parents and those within the Meeting. We were part of the Exclusive Brethren. As such, we didn't allow anyone to walk into Meeting on Lord's Day to break bread. Anybody could walk in off the street, but they had to have been received and accepted within the local Meeting or have a letter of commendation from another Meeting to break bread. This letter would vouch for their morality and good standing within their local Meeting.

For outsiders, it was important for them to understand that there was sin in the world and unrepentant sinners were not allowed to break bread. If somebody who was an accepted member, or as we referred to it as "at the Lord's

Table," was found to be guilty of adultery, fornication, drunkenness, gambling, or other significant sinful behaviors, they were ex-communicated and ostracized.

I'm not aware of an official list of sins of that magnitude, but if a person was found to be guilty of a significant sin, the Meeting-brothers would meet, discuss the situation, and if the person was judged to be guilty of significant sin, they were "put away from the Lord's Table." In doing so, they were welcome to attend the various Meetings during the week and on Lord's Day, but they were not allowed to break bread, and nobody would shake hands or talk with them. They were essentially shunned, or ostracized, and the hope was that through shunning, they would turn to the Lord and seek re-admittance to the Lord's Table by confessing their sins, and by being meek and humble. This process of re-admittance didn't take place over a few days or a week, but often lasted months. The Meeting-brothers wanted to see real evidence that the person who had been put away from the Lord's Table was contrite, really sorry for their sinful behavior, and had re-committed their life to Christ.

It wasn't until I was in my early teens that I began to notice cracks in the foundation of my parents' world, the Meeting, and the carefully constructed social structure within the Meeting. Mr. S. was put away from the Lord's Table for adultery. My parents provided no details, but news leaked out that Mr. S. had sinned and had been excommunicated. He would be ostracized. He could attend Meeting, sit in the back, and people would shun him. He and his wife had five kids. I felt sorry for them. I could see embarrassment on their faces at Meeting as he sat in the back, shunned and separate from his family.

Next, was Bill K. – his case was a surprise for me. My father said he had been "put away from the Lord's table" for fornication, although he wouldn't discuss it. Bill K. was a young, single man who had come into the Meeting from outside, and by some accounts, from a wealthy family in New York City. He was a conscientious objector to the draft and the Vietnam War. Official hearings regarding his claim as a conscientious objector (C.O.) depended on his status in the Meeting, and I remember that the Meeting-Brothers wrote a formal letter in support of his C.O. application. After he was put away for fornication, I heard my grandfather suggest that his intense interest in the Meeting might have been to provide a bona fide for his C.O. application. Certainly he was an outlier in the Meeting, neither being born into it, married into it, or being a social misfit. After he was excommunicated, he moved to Florida and was generally unheard of afterward.

Later, Uncle Jim was put away for a similar offense, adultery. His case hit me hardest. Uncle Jim wasn't really my uncle, but he was one of the adults I looked up to and respected. This was especially true because we lived an eight hour drive from our nearest relatives. To me, he was a surrogate uncle; his wife, "Aunt Sharon," a surrogate aunt. Our families spent many weekends, evenings and holidays together over the course of many years. His "fall from grace," as my father put it, was definitely a contributor to my increasing levels of skepticism. If the adults I'd looked up to during my formative years were failing, who could I count on? Had they been lying to me all this time? Was this all some sort of cosmic joke?

Despite the failings of some of the men in the Meeting who I respected, somehow the mental constructions of a universe that God had created, of Jesus who had died for my sins, and of being saved from hell, remained firmly in my mind as true. Sure, I had questions, like where did Cain's wife come from? The Bible didn't say. And people failed, they sinned; that is what had happened with Bill K., Mr. S. and Uncle Jim. Human beings were failed creatures and we had to hold fast our faith and the hope of eternal life in heaven.

After all, we in the Meeting considered ourselves to be conservators of "*the* Truth," rediscovered by J. N. Darby and held closely against the forces of evil, which included most formal religious institutions. Satan was an enemy of the Truth, a tempter of men, and there were dark forces in the world that sought to derail our endeavors to live for Christ. According to the baby book my mother kept of my childhood, I evidently believed Satan was a nasty dude: "if I see him, I'm going to hit him with a big stick," she documented me saying at age five.

Fervent faith was central to our beliefs. Skepticism was sin. Our source of truth was God's Word, the Bible. "God said it, I believe it, that finishes it!" – that was, in essence, our motto. J. N. Darby had been so concerned about discerning the true words of God, that he had translated the Bible from original Greek, Aramaic and Hebrew texts. The Meeting primarily used the King James version of the Bible, but also used Darby's translation for precise clarity whenever necessary.

Singing became a joy for me. Although no musical instruments were allowed or used in our formal Meetings, many songs are still etched in my brain. I took blissful joy from Helen Howarth Lemmel's hymn:

> "O, soul are you weary and troubled?
> No light in the darkness you see? ...
>
> Turn your eyes upon Jesus,

> Look full in his wonderful face;
> And the things of earth will grow strangely dim
> In the light of His glory and grace." [4]

Hymn sings, especially in winter, and typically on Saturday evenings at somebody's home with someone playing the piano, were warm social exchanges among Brothers and Sisters in Christ. So, there was joy and love in our social clan, even though there were clouds of doubt on the horizon.

A song we sang in Meeting, included the lines:

> "We're pilgrims in the wilderness;
> Our dwelling is a camp;
> Created things though pleasant,
> Now bear to us death's stamp"

> "With fellow-pilgrims meeting,
> As through the waste we roam;
> 'Tis sweet to sing together,
> 'We are not far from home.'" [5]

Songs like these, sung so many times during my childhood, are never far from easy recall. They reinforced that the world was full of sin, evil, pain, suffering, and we were not a part of it. Of course, we also suffered, but our suffering was buffered by the love of our Lord, Jesus Christ, and our hope for eternity with Him.

Another song we often sang on Lord's Day mornings:

> "O Christ, what burdens bowed Thy head!
> Our load was laid on Thee;
> Thou stoodest in the sinner's stead -

Didst bear all ill for me.
A Victim led, Thy blood was shed;
Now there's no load for me." [4]

I cannot read those words today without the internal, silent accompaniment of the tune that went with it, that is, I sing it as I read it. These songs don't haunt me, they are simply relics of a bygone era.

And then there was song 53 in the Appendix of our "Little Flock" hymn book:

"Alas, and did my Saviour bleed!
And did my Saviour die?
Would He devote that sacred head
For such a worm as I?" [5]

This hymn encapsulated the ideas that we were worms of the dust, unworthy of God's love, and without Christ's suffering on the cross, doomed to eternity in hell.

Essentially, we human beings were detestable! For my grandfather Harold, my father and many people like him, pride was a sin. "Pride goeth before a fall," reads Proverbs 16:18 (KJV). Harold evidently believed it to his core. And he wanted his son and his grandchildren to manifest humility, to eschew pride. These desires manifested themselves in strange ways and in strange situations. – I vividly remember visiting my brother's first wife in the hospital, soon after she gave birth to Harold's first great-grandchild. Walking into the hospital room, I was introduced to my sister-in-law's father. He was Italian and exuded genuine warmth and pleasure at meeting the brother of his son-in-law. "My what a handsome man you are!" – he exclaimed. Harold, who was also in the room, immediately stepped up behind me. "It isn't so!," he whispered in my ear. I was so taken aback at the polemical messages my ears had just registered, that I said nothing. Later, I thought about the exchange, and concluded that Harold meant well, he was just keeping me humble. Pride was a sin. Pride goeth before a fall. He wanted to keep me from falling. I was, after-all, just a worm.

5

PUNISHMENTS, CONFRONTATIONS AND VIOLENCE

I don't remember my first spanking, but I do remember my last one, which turned into a physical confrontation with my father. I also remember the last spanking my brother received; it went on for fifteen minutes or more. More accurately, it was a beating. My brother had a shrill voice when he was young and the screams coming from the downstairs living room sounded nearly inhuman. I stood at the top of the stairs giddy, quivering and sick with panic, fright, and the dawning realization that this spanking was unusual. This one smacked of desperation. – My father sensed he had lost control of his boys and this was a last-ditch effort to gain back the control he had lost over at least one of them.

Moreover, we had a visitor at our home and Mom had gone to town with my sisters. I don't remember the reason for the punishment, but it must have been especially egregious. The visitor, Walter P., was a young, single Meeting Brother in his early thirties with a near-angelic expression etched on his face, whose smile drew in people like my father. He clearly loved the Lord. He had just left the army and had carpentry skills, which my father needed, and this was the way Meeting people often operated. A person would visit us, stay with us, work for us, and we in turn would pay them, do their laundry, and provide them with good meals and a comfortable room while sharing Christian fellowship.

Anyway, the spanking my brother suffered that night was extraordinary, and I didn't know whether to laugh, cry, or go down and somehow run interference. In my early teens at the time, I feared my father and was not big enough physically to take him on, nor would the thought have seriously crossed my mind. Walter P. saw me standing at the top of the stairs, listened briefly to the carnage below, and retired to his room.

My father spanked us with a leather brush. As I remember, the brush was substantially constructed, about fifteen inches long with black bristles and a brown leather back about three-eighths of an inch thick. I have no idea of the brush's original purpose, because I never saw it used for any other purpose than to punish me and my brother. I had no idea where my father kept it, but apparently my brother did, because not long after this violent episode, the brush disappeared forever. Only years later did my brother tell me he had taken it down to the local creek and given it a violent hurl, or maybe he'd buried in the backyard; he couldn't remember.

My memory is not clear on the precedence of events, but I know that the spankings stopped for me and my brother about the time I was sixteen. I cannot imagine spanking a sixteen year old kid today, but it certainly happened to me. Once the brush disappeared, my father tried to use his hands, but that was a problem since he suffered intermittently from a case of severe eczema, which produced sores on his hands that cracked and bled. He also used a leather belt.

Perhaps the confluence of me growing bigger and stronger, the missing brush, bleeding hands, and my father's growing realization that beatings didn't really help all that much, all contributed to a cessation of the beatings. But the catalyst for change may have been a major confrontation that took place and which was a source of sorrow and regret in my family for years if not decades. This time, I had misbehaved at Meeting one particular Lord's Day morning, and following established routine, Dad told me I was going to be punished when we got home. For him, this approach was biblically correct because, first, he didn't reflexively punish me in anger, and second, but perhaps not biblically, he didn't want to create a scene in front of other people in the Meeting, although he never completely succeeded in meeting the second objective, as I'll describe later.

But on this particular Sunday, I was given *the message*, and the usual dread and sinking heart followed. To be told that you were going to be physically punished at a later time was similar to what I suspect goes on between cats and mice. I knew that there was no chance to escape the punishment, because my father never forgot. This task was on the heavenly to-do list. However, I knew if I behaved in a repentant fashion, I might attenuate the potential physical suffering I was about to endure, and in rare cases escape it entirely. However, a big part of my day was destroyed. For after the message of my forthcoming punishment was conveyed, the dread set in, and the ride home was a quiet and sometimes tearful look at the countryside. I knew I was in for it.

Clearly, my father was a fervent believer in not sparing the rod. "Train up a child in the way he should go," reads

Proverbs 22:6 (KJV), and "spare not the rod." Further, "he that spareth his rod hateth his son; but he that loveth him chasteneth him betimes" (Proverbs 13:24, KJV). But then there is the New Testament verse of Ephesians, 6:4 (KJV), "and, ye fathers, provoke not your children to wrath: but bring them up in the nurture and admonition of the Lord." In my estimation, my father failed both sets of verses. He drove his sons to wrath, and although one could argue that chastening his sons was an act of love, I would eventually conclude, based on multiple data points in time, that the love of my father and mother was conditional.

Mom always set a beautiful Sunday meal in the early afternoon. If I was lucky, the spanking would be short, swift and done before this meal. Then, with an order to wash up, I'd appear at the table still trembling with involuntary heaves and sobs, and Mom would come to me, gather me in her apron, and smooth things over; she was good at that. Her husband had her convinced, and I do believe she was convinced herself, that the God of the Bible instructed parents to reprove their children, and that included physical punishment.

My mother physically hit me only once, and she felt so bad about it that we both began crying and the motherly love she felt for me, and the love I felt for her melted us into each others' arms. I had been drying dishes for her, and evidently complaining about it, and she grabbed a wooden mixing spoon and smacked me on my back. I probably deserved it! But it stung, and I grabbed the spoon from her hand, stepped outside and hurled the offending object as far as I could.

The problem with my father's punishments is that they were generally accompanied by a solemn sermon. These could literally go on for hours. At some point I realized that a physical beating was a trifle compared to these mental beatings. They started with his expressed concern about my spiritual well-being, included recitations and readings from the Bible, and exhortations to be a follower of Christ. These were followed by us both on our knees in prayer. If I responded well, I might even get out of a spanking, but typically – although there were exceptions – the spanking was administered with little outright anger on my father's part.

The procedure was this: at some point he would announce that my spanking was to commence. He instructed me to kneel over the bed, with my back end exposed or at least my pants pulled down, and told to keep my hands out of the way. The leather brush appeared from somewhere, but in my terror I never discerned its location. And then the blows started to come, and pain and crying came with it. Typically, I don't think these spankings lasted more than a minute or two, but occasionally lasted much longer. And I remember him saying "get your hands out of the way." So, I didn't always stay still, which meant that sometimes my hands got hit instead of my ass, and then the spankings escalated into quasi-beatings as he tried to hold me in place while administering his punishment. It all depended on my infraction, and who knows what else. My father wasn't a huge guy physically, but at six feet tall and 180 pounds he was no weakling.

The orderly protocol of these spankings began to deteriorate as I grew older and physically larger. I was certainly a rebellious kid. And these were the days when long hair, peace and rebellion against the establishment were in vogue. The length of my hair was a source of constant conflict in my house, and since my father had cut his fellow soldiers' hair when he was serving as a conscientious objector in the army in Korea, he insisted on cutting mine.

Thus, the hair-related conflict was renewed about every two weeks, and I mostly lost these conflicts.

The climax of haircutting came one weekend when I told him I didn't want my hair cut and that I wasn't going to have it cut. As an alternative, I proposed going into town to a barber. But, he wasn't having it. A wrestling match ensued and I ended up on my back on the concrete floor of our basement with my father sitting on my chest and stomach, his knees pinning down my arms. My mother, hearing the commotion, asked what the matter was, whereupon she was instructed by my father to come down and to sit on my legs. She did so reluctantly and was distressed at the conflict, but my hair got cut.

I was traumatized by this event for a long time, and I don't think I immediately realized its effects. Conflict with my father and brother continued on a day-to-day basis, and I can't remember any positive experiences with my father during that period. There was never any play, no throwing a ball or frisbee, only the Meeting and lots of Bible reading and prayer. So, I was dominated physically and coerced mentally to attend Meeting, and my father constrained my behavior by outlasting me and out-maneuvering me physically. I recall my rebellion keeping us from leaving for vacations, with me out in the yard while everybody else sat in the car waiting for me to surrender. Since these events occurred out in front of the neighbors in full daylight, my father left me alone.

For years after the pinning incident, I had a repeating nightmare wherein I'd wake up terrified at being smothered by a giant frog sitting on me, choking off my air supply. I couldn't move, I couldn't breathe, I could only struggle, and I'd wake up yelling, panicked, in a hot sweat, gasping for air, my arms flailing. I didn't relate these nightmares to being pinned down by my father until years later, when I was in a counseling session where the psychologist made the connection. "It's tantamount to rape," he said. I couldn't agree with him then and still don't, because rape is altogether more heinous. But it was absolute physical dominance of a young boy by his adult-father for reasons that in retrospect seem trivial. Of course, the underlying reasons were steeped in authoritarianism, control, domination and religious fervor. I was a child and would obey, period. Witnessing and hearing these physical beatings traumatized my youngest sister, who is fourteen years younger than I am. She says the worst events happened "way more than once." Today, she avoids confrontation at all costs and attributes her stance to witnessing these events.

There was at least once when our physical violence, or threats of it, was witnessed by other people from the Meeting. One Saturday evening we had the C.-family over for dinner with their two young children. At some point after dinner, my father and I started to argue about something, or I behaved in a way that he disapproved. He took off his belt. I took off mine. I wasn't going to be punished and humiliated in front of an audience. What followed was a nasty combination of insults, crying, praying, and indignation. Mr. C. was visibly upset at "how sinful and disobedient you boys are." – I don't remember specific details of how the evening ended, but the C.-family left, and I remember being sent to my room and told to "reflect on my awful behavior."

The last time my father attempted to spank me, we fought physically; this was a major confrontation. It occurred upstairs in my brother's bedroom early on a Sunday afternoon. My brother and I were fighting, and my father got in the middle to stop the fighting and to punish us for fighting. – What happened next was a fight broke out between me and my dad. This is the only time I remember fighting violently with my father, in the sense that both of us had our fists up and we were exchanging blows. To give my father some credit, I think some of his fists-up posture was partly to protect himself. But blows flew from both directions. Filled with anger, I attacked, hitting him repeatedly with closed fists. I was blind with fury. After my anger subsided, I remember quickly feeling absolute despair, both from seeing my father crying at what had happened, his absolute acceptance of his inability to fix it, and me crying at the realization that somehow I had overcome his physical dominance by my own physicality, ferocity and rage.

Ten years after this incident my father told me I cracked one of his ribs that day. It's not a fact I'm proud of, but an indicator of the depths of physical violence to which we had sunk. Ironically, other than a scuffle with a classmate in sixth grade and fights with my brother at about that time, I've never fought physically with another person.

Another notable, yet terrifying altercation occurred a couple of years later after we moved just over the border into Pennsylvania. At this point, my father no longer attempted to spank me; I was eighteen after-all. One night, after working the evening shift, I partied with a couple of friends and arrived home around midnight. Slipping quietly into my basement bedroom, I was getting ready to go to sleep when my father knocked at the door. Once again, he expressed his adamant disapproval at the way I was living my life, and an argument escalated, getting louder and trending toward violence. I felt my private life off the premises of the family home was my own business; my father disagreed. He contended that this was a Christian home and I was not abiding by his rules.

By now, we had fought so often that the strife followed a

now-established pattern of quick escalation. My brother, still in the next room, insists that this one escalated to the point that he heard my father choking me. Soon after, my bedroom door was kicked open from the outside and my brother, fourteen, stood there with a shotgun pointed directly at my father.

My mother, who had been sitting on the stairs that came down from the kitchen, said "Charles, come upstairs." My father's face turned ashen, you could visibly see it, and he went up the stairs without another word. I don't remember anything ever being said about this episode. My father confiscated the gun the following day. Soon after, my brother left home. At age fourteen, it wasn't the first time he had left. I think the level of intra-familial conflict was too much for him, and leaving home for a few days was his way of attempting to cope with a physically dominant father.

I personally never witnessed my father physically punish my sisters, but one of my sisters says: "I remember receiving two very hard spankings from Dad, and at eighteen, being smacked across the face because I was angry with him." My other sister has withheld comment.

My father wasn't the only father in the Meeting to mete out physical punishment. Spankings, and other physical punishments, were mostly the norm. For example, I overheard Russell R. tell my father he used a ping-pong paddle as his chosen spanking instrument, one he had customized by drilling holes in "to make it sting more" when it struck flesh or pants. Belts were a popular means of meting out punishments, as were slaps, the latter being useful for ad-hoc situations since no effort was necessary to retrieve an appropriate weapon.

Actually witnessing one of these events was relatively rare. However, one Sunday morning at Meeting during

breaking of bread, Jim P. picked up little Suzie, who had
been misbehaving, by one arm, opened the door and
spanked her all the way down the stairs. She must have
been five at the time. We all heard the smacks and squeals
of pain as he descended the stairwell.

Then there was the time when we were driving to
Greenwood Park with the S. family. My father always
bought used cars, and he was driving an older Dodge station
wagon with the rear, third seat facing backward.

It was a beautiful sunny day and most of the windows in
the car were open, including the back one. Mr. and Mrs. S.
were sitting in the back seat, and my brother and I were
sitting in the far-back seat facing out back, with the oldest S.
boy, David, who was about twelve years old at the time.
David was telling a joke to my brother and me that included
the word "shit." When his father overheard it, he reached
around the seat and violently backhanded David in the face.
I vividly remember the smack and David's glasses flying out
the back window, landing on the road. We had to pull over
and back up to retrieve them.

David had a cut on his nose and was crying with sobs
and heaves that seemed to involuntarily overtake his body. I
couldn't blame him; he had been viciously assaulted.
Although I have it only on rumor, although from a credible
source, I hear that David is as strict a father today as his
father was then. Hearing such news is humorous, dismaying
and sickening to me, because Mr. S. eventually left his wife
with their five children, moved in with another woman and
was put away from the Lord's table. How David could grow
up in such an environment, experience the abandonment
by his father, and yet still be a strict, conservative Christian
is, for me, an ongoing puzzle.

But, my surrogate uncle, Uncle Jim, probably took the

prize for the most violent of punishments and resulting injuries. After one notable spanking episode, his daughter Sheila had welts, cuts and bruises to such an extent that she couldn't sit for almost two weeks. And it wasn't just a one-and-done. The wounds were carefully positioned such that they didn't show beneath the hemlines of the dresses she and her sisters wore to school. I heard this specific episode recounted by both Jim, who was telling the story with a chuckle to my father, and by Sheila herself. Jim definitely stood out from the rest, in terms of the violence of his punishments, and by the fact that they were administered to his girls.

Jim's adamant, fanatical demeanor manifested itself in many ways. One of his daughters told me that he built a coffin out of plywood, and trimmed it out in green and white. He placed it in their bedroom beneath a window where they would see it when they looked out at the world. He did it to remind them that they were "dead to the world, but alive unto God."

Jim also appeared to be an expert at shunning. Several times he literally turned his back on people he judged were not "walking in the ways of the Lord." I witnessed this behavior with my own eyes. It was supposedly a form of Christian love. And this is the guy who subsequently left his wife and six children and moved in with another woman, leaving the Meeting and abandoning everything for which he had once fanatically stood. My thoughts of him and his fanatical religiosity are now steeped in derision.

6

INTRODUCING BUD

As I grew up, I became aware that my father had a brother, his only living sibling. Robert, or Bud as my father called him, lived in Basel, Switzerland and worked as a medical researcher for a large pharmaceutical company. After earning an M.D. in the United States, he had been drafted and sent to Europe, working in the army as a pathologist. He evidently liked Europe so much, he stayed.

Bud was a mysterious figure in our family, at least to me. I heard my father talk about Bud to their father, my grandfather Harold. Bud, like my father, had grown up in the Meeting under what was later described to me as an authoritarian and disciplinarian environment; very similar to mine. From what I heard as a teenager, Bud no longer considered himself a Christian, and that led to a schism in the family. My father generally kept his letters to and from Bud private or only read what he considered acceptable content to us over the dinner table. In doing so, he inadvertently increased my curiosity about his relationship with Bud, which appeared to repeatedly wax and wane over time.

As far as I could tell, Bud had little to no relationship with their father, and the familial schism seemed to center on religion. But this controversy was mostly kept from me and my siblings.

One letter Bud wrote to my father in 1966, centered on the differences in beliefs between him and my father.

"I spent nine years of my life as a pathologist. I performed autopsies on 600 bodies, ranging from centenarians to premature babies. I served as expert witness in three murder investigations, one of which involved a baby killed by its own parents. If I feel a bit uncomfortable about the women and children (and men) being burned up every day by Napalm [in Vietnam], it may be because I have been obliged to perform too many autopsies on bodies consisting primarily of charcoal (or of soap, after weeks in a river). When I am told that God is all-powerful and all-good at the same time, the message doesn't get through to me."

Clearly, this excerpt was never read to me or my siblings; we were quite young at the time and my youngest sister hadn't yet been born.

Bud would eventually become a mentor to me during my late twenties. However, in my teens, there were significant levels of fighting and strife within my family, most specifically between me and my father but also involving my younger brother. Simultaneously, although I was unaware, Bud and my father, Charles, were exchanging letters and cassette tapes with increasing frequency, the conversation had become heated, and I and my brother were a central theme.

One direct result of the conflict between me and my

father was that about the time I turned eighteen, I was forced to leave home. My mother had discovered some poorly concealed issues of Penthouse magazine underneath a carpet beneath my bed, and I was partying with friends using cannabis and alcohol. I had graduated early from high school and was working a full-time job. But my father made adamantly clear that his was a Christian home. As such, a person who looked at Penthouse and used cannabis would not be tolerated. So, barely eighteen, out I went, moving into town.

Bud died in April 1999 of Parkinson's disease. In June 1999, I was invited by his and my father's first cousin, Stu, who lived in northern Europe, to travel to Basel and go through Bud's belongings. Bud kept a trunk full of letters and related correspondence in storage, accumulated over his life. Immensely curious, I did my best to go through them, shipping several boxes of these intercontinental missives and other keepsakes back to my home in the USA.

My father's message in a cassette tape I recovered in Basel after Bud's death, was that his boys were misbehaving. My father began his recording by stating "our two boys are not living at home." Dan left a few months ago, soon after turning eighteen, and Dwight, fourteen, left one month later. "It came to the point," he said, "where Dan started coming home late; out in the evening, returning in the morning hours. I'm not going to say all that I've found out that Dan was involved in, some things that were wrong by the standards of this world, of this society, and I spoke to Dan, and Dan did not respond. And I told him that he could not live in our house ... and go on in the way that he was. This is a Christian home and you cannot go on in wrong ways. And so, he moved out."

He continued: "Dwight is different. He has been antagonistic; very rebellious. He's run away from home several times. Not very far; yet we didn't know how far. We had to call the police because he was gone overnight; we didn't know where he was. He has been gone for several days at a time, on several occasions. He's been openly hateful toward me."

Dwight, at fourteen, refused to go to Meeting or attend school, and the law compelled parents to ensure that children under age sixteen attended school. After months of fighting, with my father calling the police on several occasions when my brother didn't attend school, a local judge removed my brother from my parents' legal custody. He then moved in with a family down the road, to which my parents made monthly custody payments. About one month earlier, I was asked to leave home because of the Penthouse-magazines discovery and my parents' disapproval of my social connections and use of alcohol and cannabis. In my defense, the alcohol and cannabis use never occurred at home, but yes, I did have copies of Penthouse in my bedroom.

"At this point," my father continued in his tape, "I finally took Dwight to a psychologist, and we also consulted with a family friend who was a probation officer. In the first visit, the psychologist confirmed to me what the probation officer said, that Dwight would leave home. And the psychologist said I'm the one that needed the help." – "So here I am in some crazy way, trying to piece together a story that I don't fully understand myself."

"However, I do want to say, without any hesitation," my father continued, "that our hope and trust is in the Lord, acknowledging all our need and all our failure, certainly not blaming the Lord for all our failure. I certainly feel that although the psychologist hasn't opened up the page of a book and shown me some new revelation that I haven't seen before, I can see that I'm very controlling, very strong in my role as a father, and trying to make my children conform to my ideas. I acknowledge my failures. I have been a disciplinarian. And I'm sure that this touches you because of your own problems that you've experienced with [our father Harold]; I also."

He continued... "I don't know what to think of this psychologist-business. I took my boy to the psychologist, and the psychologist said you're the guy that has all the defenses; you're the guy I need to work with. He wants to work with Dwight, but the problem that he recognizes is with me; he said, 'don't expect to see a big change in Dwight until the change comes in you!'"

The contents of this tape from my father to his brother, my Uncle Bud, apparently did not sit well with Bud. He and my father had both been recipients of similar treatment from their own father, Harold. Like my father, Harold was also a Christian fanatic, and as a father, over-controlling and a harsh disciplinarian. The difference, of course, is that my father had followed in his own father's footsteps, whereas Bud, after years of introspection and discovery had gone in the opposite direction. Bud had recorded two tapes in response to my father's, one of which was sent and, as I was to find out years later, significantly offended my father. "It was full of swearing" he said, "I threw it away."

Bud never mailed this second tape, which is why I discovered it so many years later among his belongings in Basel. In it, Bud apologized for his strong language in his first tape and promised to try to attenuate his reaction to the contents of my father's tape, and make his message less offensive.

After a few apologies, Bud said "I have a feeling that

these boys are reacting to you. You call yourself a disciplinarian, and that's probably a euphemism, since I strongly
suspect that they are reacting more to the sense that they
aren't getting the truth from you, just as [our father]
continues to swindle me about the truth today. It's not possible, I assume, for someone who has taken up a life pattern
as [our father], and you also have largely done, to deal with
truth directly. I'm not claiming that I can do it; I can only
claim that I do everything I can to try."

"My feeling is very strong that these boys, two very
different personalities, think there ain't no god-damned
whole truth to what [you, their father] is talking about. But
the fact that each boy retains some contact with you indi-
cates that you have come a lot further than [our father] ever
came with me, and have been able to at least convince them
that you are willing to talk. – Whether you are willing to
open your mind is another question!"

Bud continued, "I think this is the question that these
two boys at their own levels, with their various characters,
experiences, and different ages are asking themselves right
now. That's why this tape, like the last one, has a rather
pleading tone. In the name of Christ, be kind to these boys!
And not kind in the sense of giving them chicken pie or
whatever the hell kind of pie you want to give them. Tell
them what you feel! Say that you're not sure of yourself. Say
that what you are telling them is what you believe, but that
you can't speak for God!"

"I have a very strong feeling, Charles, this is what they
are feeling and when you describe your home as a Christian
home instead of your own home, I can't imagine any other
reaction from these boys except total rejection." – "I hope
this [cassette tape] will be less painful, although intention-
ally at least will be equally direct, and motivated at the

conscious level for the purpose of getting you to realize that human beings at whatever age are individuals and can't be treated as if they are born slaves, as our father treated me."

"But you, Charles, should have a pretty good idea of what I'm talking about. – I'm expressing the hope that by telling you this, you might still save something in your relationships with your boys. – I'm telling you what I think because everything else is worthless."

"You've told me that Dan left home. But my interpretation from your tape is that you kicked him out! If that's the case, you probably justified this based on your own Christian principles, but whether they are justified at the human level is not clear from your tape, to put it mildly. And I ask you very bluntly, my brother Charles, is it worthwhile being a Christian but no god-damned human being?! I'm sorry to have to be so violent about this, but I don't see our father as being a fully functional human being. I don't think he ever was. He certainly never will be from my point of view."

"Human beings are people who react to other human beings at the human level. And if something like religion comes first, then the person who allowed this to happen degrades himself, in my opinion, to something less than human. And I speak so strongly because I fear you have gone the wrong way in this direction and can only imagine that the loss of your two boys – not the total loss, but loss in some real sense – is in your case, not entirely irreparable if you are willing to come down off your god damned Mount Sinai with the tables of law glowing, like Moses."

At the time these cassette letters were exchanged, I had no knowledge of their existence or their contents. Little did I know my uncle was defending me and my brother from a continent away, from a fanatic who claimed to know the truth, and as a result felt justified to force his truth on his children. In retrospect, perhaps Bud could have been kinder in his approach, but given the unmovable object, that of my father's stubborn belief for which he had no evidence, and my uncle's experience of dealing with a similar tyrant from the previous generation in the form of his father, I view his anger and bluntness justified.

7

ON MY OWN

When I was sixteen, Dad and Mom sold our house in New York, and moved to seventeen mostly wooded acres across the border in Pennsylvania. Soon after, I bought my first car to commute to my New York high school to finish my studies. I had all the credits I needed to graduate, and finished in December of my final year, graduating six months earlier than my peers. – I never went back. I didn't participate in graduation, never bought a yearbook, and didn't keep in contact with any of my peers with whom I had spent significant portions of the previous twelve-plus years. Perhaps I associated many of those years with the authoritarian and disciplinarian climate at home. But because I wasn't allowed to engage in any extracurricular activities at school over the course of those twelve years, I felt like a social outcast and misfit.

A couple of months later, I landed a job with a large industrial company. I worked at various jobs in the warehouse, then assembly, then trained as a quality inspector and worked in quality assurance. Having my own money and transportation enabled me to move out of my family home soon after I turned eighteen. One could argue over whether I voluntarily left home or whether I had been kicked out. Regardless, out I went.

During the next few months, I stayed away from family, away from the Meeting, and developed ties with a few people who became friends. Some of these friendships were with neighborhood kids from our former home in New York. Cannabis and alcohol were part of the milieu, and helped me cope with my lack of social skills.

I still saw my family, but only irregularly. Whenever I went home, there was typically a heated argument with my father. But relatively little physical violence.

I shifted between hanging out and partying with friends, and returning home with a goal to straighten out my life. At some point, I began to attend Meeting again. I wanted to make something of my life, and partying wasn't getting me anywhere. Moreover, I wanted God to approve of my life. – And, while I didn't believe that my father's strict interpretation of the Bible and his fanatical close-mindedness about so many issues were correct, I was determined to find a path forward that I could live with, a path I described as "middle-of-the-road."

So, I set aside the legalized climate of the Meeting, with its rules and strict biblical interpretation. I felt this path would allow me to live in the world, to find my own way, to pursue happiness and not feel guilty about it; a path that preserved my faith in God, but wasn't so constricting that I couldn't enjoy life. Moreover, I didn't want to fanatically immerse myself in all things biblical on a daily basis. I had done that for so long via the adamant indoctrination from my parents, that it seemed more like a duty, even self-torture, than a joy or a passion.

Looking back, and relating to my younger self, I can

fully relate to the feelings expressed by Edmund Gosse in his classic book, *Father and Son,*[1] where he says "whether the facts and doctrines contained in the Bible were true or false was not the question that appealed to me; it was rather that they had been presented to me so often and had sunken into me so far that, as someone has said, they 'lay bedridden in the dormitory of the soul,' and made no impression of any kind upon me."

Thus, I was happy that the Lord, Jesus Christ would come back to earth some day, but I wasn't yet ready for heaven. I had things to do! And, I was restless; the territory of the New York-Pennsylvania border was not where I wanted to be. I wanted to travel. And I wanted distance from my family.

What happened next? I moved back home for a few short months and became attracted to a young woman in the Meeting. We married a few months later. She was in her late teens; I was twenty; what could go wrong? – The marriage lasted quite a few years, but ultimately dissolved. She didn't have the religious questions that plagued me, nor was she interested in them. She stayed out of familial arguments about religion. Thoughts of eternity and its definitional characteristic of infinity terrified her and she would not discuss it. She had grown up outside the Meeting and had come into it through her sister, who also married a Meeting-boy. Her father viewed the Meeting as a cult, and disapproved of it, although he eventually became quite religious and quite insufferable as a result.

Just short of two years after the wedding, we quit our jobs, sold some of our belongings, and stored the remainder in my parents' barn. We headed west, toward a landscape of which I had dreamed all my life, the Rocky Mountains. Although my parents had not allowed a TV or radio inside the family home, and this was pre-internet, they had allowed me to borrow books from the library, and didn't check too much as to their titles or content, although my father constantly reminded me to "keep your focus on things above," that is, on God and heaven. Some of the books I read were of the western variety, with descriptions of mountains, canyons, and vast open spaces. I also purchased and voraciously read *Western Horseman* magazine.

The first time I saw the Rocky Mountains in Colorado, something clicked in my brain; I knew I was home. I felt it mentally, spiritually and physically. The wide-open spaces, the smell of Ponderosa pines, the quaking aspens, the drama of the peaks and the sheer wildness of the mountain landscape captured me like nothing before!

The fights and disagreements with my parents faded into the background, unresolved. My wife and I worked at various jobs, moved around to several locations in Colorado, made brief months-long stays in Idaho, and even returned to Pennsylvania for several months before recommitting to Colorado. After a few years, we moved to southwest Colorado. There I began taking courses at Fort Lewis College (FLC) in Durango.

FLC was and is a four-year liberal arts school, staffed with talented professors who care. They could have been teaching at schools that provided more lucrative salaries and more recognition of their research, but these would have lacked FLC's student-centered culture and the recreational opportunities and lifestyle provided by Durango's stunning location.

I took courses in art, physics, statics, semantics (thanks Professor Paul Pavich!), history, philosophy, math, economics, business and many more. I worked hard and excelled in my studies. I quit my full-time job as a water treatment plant operator, found a part-time job with the Durango & Silverton Narrow Gauge Railroad, and attended college full-time. By then, I was technically a non-traditional student, being a few years older than my undergraduate peers, but I felt this status was a strength: I knew something of the outside world, had work experience and loved my studies.

My father looked on from a distance with concern. Years before he had told me that "Jesus was a carpenter and that should be good enough for you." And while I enjoyed building things, college was calling; almost an imperative. Without a college education I felt incomplete. My father's only sibling, Bud, had gone to the University of Michigan, then on to medical school, eventually becoming a Medical Doctor. Somewhere along the way, Bud had discarded much of his strict, fundamentalist Plymouth Brethren-based religious upbringing, for something different, which he viewed as an improvement, but which was looked upon with sick-dismay by my father, and their father Harold. My father reminded me of the Bible verse, Acts 26:24 (KJV), where Festus says to Paul, "thou art beside thyself; much learning doth make thee mad." The New American Standard Bible translation says, "Paul, you are out of your mind! Your great learning is driving you mad." Apparently Paul disagreed with that assessment, saying "I am not out of my mind.... But I utter words of sober truth." Regardless, my father and my grandfather Harold causally associated Bud's years of higher education with his becoming an atheist, and they were concerned I might follow in my uncle's footsteps.

As I proceeded through my studies at FLC, I thought a lot about life and what I hoped to do with mine. I still believed in God and wondered what He wanted me to do. I took a philosophy course and tentatively asked the professor if he believed in God. He replied that he attended church every Sunday. That was a good sign; evidently he wouldn't turn me into an atheist. I was afraid of that.

Actually, I was afraid of God! On the one hand, Jesus loved me; on the other, hell and eternal torment awaited people who didn't accept Him as Savior. So, I took the course and walked away with mixed feelings about the field of philosophy. We had studied Socrates, Kant, Plato, Decartes, and some of the writings of William James. But the class left me unfulfilled. Yes, rational argument and logical thought applied to the big questions of life were worthwhile. But where were the conclusions I could apply to my life? And where was God? Did He exist? Did He care? Would He punish me for doubting what my parents had taught me?

During the final year of my undergraduate studies, I typed out a letter to my Uncle Bud. Clearly my father had taken full advantage of his chances with me during my youth and young adulthood to instill in me a fear and love of God, but what was it with sin? Was sin solely a religious concept? Were sin and evil the same thing? Why were things the way they are? Why were lions obligatory carnivores, imposing suffering and death on other animals to stay alive? Why did we have to wait until that time period described in the biblical book of Revelations when lambs would lie peacefully with lions? Why was being gay such an abhorrent sin? And anyway, what was sin? Why was the Old Testament filled with so much violence? And, why wasn't the New Testament not much better? If God so loved the world, as it stated in John 3:16, why did He create hell?

My formal education was going well, but the beliefs that had dominated my life from the womb were littered with questions. I was supposed to have faith, and to doubt was sinful, but the suffering of the human race and of animals filled me with doubts.

When I first moved to Colorado, I took jobs that involved water treatment and related maintenance activities at a couple of small towns. The first job, especially, involved me spending several days throughout the year behind the wheel of a large road grader. While grading dirt roads, I had plenty of time to think in full view of the front range of the majestic Rocky Mountains. Those mountains inspired me. They made me think of God, who I believed had created them. They made me think of that verse in Jeremiah 29:13 (KJV), "And ye shall seek me, and find me, when ye shall search for me with all your heart."

I did search with all my heart. My parents had tried to inculcate in me a love for God, but this was me as a lone adult, searching for truth as best I could ascertain it. Over the course of a couple of years, I kept returning to the Bible. Verses that inspired me included, Ephesians 1, verses 3-4 (KJV), "Blessed be the God and Father of our Lord Jesus Christ, who hath blessed us with all spiritual blessings in heavenly places in Christ: According as He hath chosen us in Him before the foundation of the world..." By then, I no longer believed, as my father once had, that the earth was ~6,000 years old. The verse in II Peter 3:8 (KJV), "one day is with the Lord as a thousand years, and a thousand years as one day," sort of shot down young-earth theory. And unless one believed, as some people I knew, that God or Satan put fossils on earth to confuse geologists, clearly the earth was very old, perhaps, according to scientists and their data, billions of years.

Whatever one believed, those verses in Ephesians meant, to me, that before the earth existed, God knew about me, knew I would believe in Him, and had "chosen" me to spend eternity in heaven with Him! Thinking about that gave me chills. It was incomprehensible, almost, to think that God so loved me, so loved the world (John 3:16) that before I existed, He knew of my upcoming presence on earth and wanted me to be with Him for all eternity. I reveled in that verse as a backdrop against all of life's troubles, until one day I thought, "well, what about those he didn't choose?"

In retrospect, I think the level of my reservoir of faith, if one can think about it that way, started to significantly decline that day. At the very least it took some joy out of my belief. What about all those people who weren't saved? Sure, murderers, rapists, pedophiles and other people who committed the most grievous sins, probably deserved eternity in hell. But the Bible said "all have sinned and come short of the glory of God" (Romans 3:23). That meant everybody had sinned and would be going to hell unless they believed in Jesus and God (John 3:16). My father's business card, which he handed out at every opportunity, put it very succinctly, "the wages of sin is death, but the gift of God is eternal life through Jesus Christ our Lord" (Romans 6:23, KJV).

Approaching my uncle was an act of rebellion, in some sense, because my father didn't approve of him as a source of valid knowledge or truth. My father and my grandfather were clearly upset by Bud's beliefs; his beliefs appeared to be counter to everything they believed. But I had to find out. What had created such a schism in my family's previous generation? What did Bud believe that seemed so horrifying to my grandfather and father? If Bud was so intelligent, as my father and grandfather seemed to imply, why did his search for truth seem so dangerous to them?

Would my uncle even answer me? If so, what would he say?

My early letters to Bud were quite tentative. I hadn't seen him since I had sat on his lap as a young child. I introduced myself, told him of my studies, my life and stated that "no subject was taboo for me." After-all, what was the point of constructing fences, separating out acceptable territory from forbidden territory? I wanted blunt honesty. At this point in my life, I had traveled out of the United States only to Canada, Mexico, and the Bahamas. Switzerland and Europe seemed like, and were for me, a foreign country and region. That my uncle, who had grown up in Detroit with my father, had moved to Europe and rarely if ever returned to the USA, was curious to me. Why had he left the United States? Why had he stayed in Europe? And, why, in his first letters did he suggest he had no desire to return?

8

ON THE CHARACTERS OF JESUS AND YAHWEH

I first wrote to Bud near the end of the 1980s. He responded in early 1989. Over the holidays, he had been visiting his and my father's first cousin, Stu, who lived in northern Europe. He was part of my father's and Bud's generation. I didn't recall meeting him, although I knew I had met him at Bible Conferences we attended when I was a kid, especially since one was typically held in Wheaton, IL, near his family home. Our common ancestors were my father's and Bud's mother, Edna, and Stu's mother, who we called Aunt Fran, who were sisters. These sisters were the children of Albert L., who had been an esteemed "Laboring Brother" in the Meeting. Laboring brothers, as I noted earlier, were traveling spiritual leaders who were financially supported by donations received from the various Meetings they visited.

In answer to my letter, Bud started by saying that "having been raised in a family and tradition in which questions are misdemeanors and opinions crimes, it means a great deal to me to find those of your generation willing to take the risk of establishing and then cultivating contact" and "not writing me off as simply an oddball and compulsive rebel."

At this time, I was in the final year of my undergraduate studies at Fort Lewis College. Bud hadn't been aware of my studies, and remarked that "my opinion is that a large amount of human effort is wasted doing things that would better not be done, thinking thoughts rooted in ignorance (i.e., avoidable ignorance), and fearing things which even a modicum of knowledge of the comparably easily available sort would dispel." In his view, "knowledge is morally and ethically value-free ... the more the better."

In this first letter Bud said he would "sketch out for you where you are likely to find me if you start looking," noting that "in American policy the communist phobia is so undifferentiated that any fascist is preferred to any with even a suspicion of 'communism' about him." He mentioned Reagan, who was about to finish his second term, stating "he encumbered his successors with incredible debts, largely for military procurement, while stopping such domestic programs as benefited the paupers, such as the school lunch program. – This is conservatism with a vengeance." He closed by saying that "my purpose in criticizing the USA so directly is primarily to offer you a contact surface not directly connected with family or religion to use as a probe."

Bud's letter simultaneously surprised, delighted and scared me. I had expected him to challenge me and my ways of thinking. And, given my background knowledge of his significant disagreements with my father and his father, Charles and Harold, I sensed that what he might convey to me would in many ways be counter to what I had been taught. But I also sensed a level of familial love and kindness that came through in his writing. I wanted to know more!

I did not answer him until December 1992. By then, I

had finished my undergraduate degree, moved to Arizona, finished a Master's degree, and started working on a social sciences doctorate.

I continued to have nagging questions regarding my beliefs, and the basis on which those beliefs rested. And there were topics that continued to plague me. Why, if the book of Genesis was true, did mankind have to suffer so much because of a simple act of disobedience, that of Eve and Adam eating a piece of fruit? If God was omniscient, all-knowing, and thus knew how evil man was going to be, "He repenteth him of the evil" (Joel 2:13, KJV), why did he put the tree in the Garden of Eden, knowing its fruit would be picked, especially when, according to the Bible, he knew that at a later time He would flood the earth, drowning every living thing except for those who made it onto Noah's ark? If God was love, was this an act of love? Why, if homosexuality was such an abomination (and it was considered an abomination by many church leaders in the 1990s, and even today), did scientific evidence propose that homosexuality was at least partly genetic and recognize that homosexuality occurs in nature? Why did prominent televangelists like Pat Robertson, who claimed to speak for God, hatefully blame hurricanes and other natural events on homosexuals? And, why did God create obligatory carnivores, such as lions, that require the suffering and death of other living animals to survive?

Underlying many of these questions was the topic of cruelty, suffering and the character of the God I had been brought up to fear and unconditionally worship. Why did so many people and animals suffer from cruel diseases like cancer? And, what did these questions mean in the face of the loving God portrayed in John 3:16? Why was I still struggling with these issues in adulthood? Was I afraid of something?

So, in late 1992, I apologized for taking so long to answer him. Updating him on my life, I wrote, rather disjointedly, "I have attended Meeting fewer than five times and various churches only a few more times than that."

I continued, saying "as you might imagine, I was raised in an environment that involved total immersion in the Meeting and all that it stands for. As the saying goes, 'too much of anything is bad,' and this, I believe, applies to religion as well. Today, I value a middle-of-the-road approach to life, i.e., zealots, religious and otherwise, scare me because their biases tend to skew their thinking, and thus their actions." I closed, repeating that "no subject is taboo for me."

He wrote back! "Your superb letter arrived just a few hours ago," he wrote, "and my pleasure at learning this door, too, is still open prompts me to try to write a few lines without waiting for time for a 'definitive' answer. – I plan to take you at your own words: 'no subject is taboo for me.'"

He continued: "So, what I'd like to do is fix on paper certain guidelines which in my view have stood the test of the decades, and in history, of the centuries. – The problem, for me, starts with the concept of truth, or 'truth' as I would put it. The attitude to this concept immediately divides people, as I see it, into two categories: believers (at this point it doesn't matter what the belief is) and skeptics. The believer begins with a proposition which pleases him, refuses to tolerate views which conflict in any way with his own, and refuses to discuss his own, although he will not fault himself for preaching at you on each and every possible occasion. Our cousin, who lives in northern

Europe, formulates this position very pointedly: 'my mind is made up, don't confuse me with facts!'"

He continued ... "the history of the conflict between 'science' and 'religion' regarding the interpretation of the book of Genesis is a clear case in point. If you ask a believer what he makes of dinosaurs, for example, he will likely give one of several stereotype answers depending on his temperament and his assessment of your, the inquirer's, sincerity. In this case usually he will avoid 'one day is with the Lord as a thousand years, and a thousand years as one day' because he has learned that no multiple of a millennium will ever explain dinosaurs, or any other futile products of nature such as rabies or AIDS viruses, for example, and perhaps console himself with some version of: 'HE [God] understands; it is not given to us to know.' At this point, if it hasn't been done earlier, the concept of 'sin' is usually introduced, or 'the blessed Lord.'"

"The skeptic, on the other hand, rejects 'magic thinking' because, among other defects, it invariably leads to unkindness at the least and, at worst, to overt cruelty including war, usually fought 'for God and country.' My own position is roughly: 'by their fruits ye shall know them,' and given that premise, no religious view has any chance with me anymore."

Bud's entrance, from a distant sideline into my intellectual life was like having a family member, friend, mentor and professor in one person. Years before, he had grappled with the same existential problems that were plaguing me. I found his letters fascinating, disturbing, provocative and potentially life changing.

In my previous letter to Bud, I had stated that I didn't tow the strict fundamentalist's line that my father (his brother) did. – "I think I understand what you mean by choosing a middle course," he said, "especially when what you are emphasizing is the avoidance of extremes, which is or are the natural homelands of fanatics. If people thought clearly on this matter, the very term 'fanatic' (which in my private usage includes fundamentalists of every sort, not only Christians) would be self-disqualifying. This is obviously not the case, so I think it wise to build in some protection by assigning fanatics to the lunatic fringe and ignoring them (not as individuals, of course, but as adherents of movements) in geometric assessment of the situation. If you are driving along the edge of a precipice, every inch you add to your distance from the edge is a distinct gain."

Well, we agreed on something, at least. Clearly, I had removed myself from the fanatical spiritual homeland inhabited by my parents and grandfather. I had found their legalized approach to life, their adamant, daily focus on the Bible and what they believed was Christ's teachings too confining and limiting for my personal use. Had Bud found a way of living that was less restrictive yet preserved my basic beliefs?

In Bud's next letter, he focused, in part, on ethics: "This subject is particularly important for one who has turned away from a fanatical position forced on him by a 'loving' family. When it became evident to me that the Judeo-Christian ethical system, cited by its defenders as the great glory of Christianity, is based on the character and opinions of the Jewish tribal god Jehovah, or Yahweh, whose character in my eyes is directly comparable among contemporaries with those of, say Saddam Hussein or Mobutu, I realized I'd have to find an ethical system of my own and succeeded after many years of effort. Without describing the process and the dozens of dead ends I got into, I'll simply give you the result. It is: 'don't exploit other people. Basta!'"

I must admit that at the time, this letter really upset me. I had told Bud that no topic was out of bounds. But here he was comparing the God of the Old Testament to murderous despots! I paused to reflect on this point for several months. I still believed in God, or some kind of god, and my university experiences had reinforced in me a thirst for knowledge.

However, Bud helped me in describing his own intellectual journey: "One result of these studies was learning to take history in its own terms instead of rewriting it to accommodate modern prejudices. If you look at the character of Jesus in this way, it turns out, for me, that it is necessary to re-evaluate him radically. 'I came not to send peace, but a sword,' Jesus says in Matthew 10:34, KJV. I think my parents put this in their category: 'you'll understand that when you're older.' They didn't even need a category for 'the poor ye have always with you, but me ye have not always' (Matthew 26:11, KJV), for it seemed self-evident to them. But when you realize what that means, especially what poverty means today, and meant in Jesus' time, it calls for long and anguished reflection. His attitude towards poverty seems to have been: 'I'm poor myself, and besides, only the afterlife counts.'"

Bud also wrote directly about Jesus and sex: "Sexuality, as far as I can see, was a big bore for him, and he tended to treat it as something of a nuisance which had to be dealt with directly so he could get on to more useful themes. 'So, you found this woman in the very act of adultery, did you, and Moses says in the law that such should be stoned, does he, well I say, let him among you who is without sin start the execution.' Marvelous psychology but no horror at 'sin or sex.' 'Woman, didn't *anybody* condemn you?' 'Well, neither do I but please don't do it again.'"

"Once as I recall, he actually did take up the subject of

sex without having to be goaded into it, in Matthew's version of the 'Sermon on the Mount': 'You have heard from the ancients not to commit adultery, but I say, whoever looks lustfully at a woman has already committed adultery with her in his heart.' Logically, in this view, and mine too, 99+% of our race is adulterous, which is perhaps the reason it doesn't count as a crime *anymore* in western jurisprudence, although it certainly did when the church had Europe in its claws. And after this brief but profound comment, he drops the subject and goes on as if he had never even raised it!"

"But Paul," he continued, "who wrote most of the New Testament, is another case altogether. Give him a chance exposure and he is off in all directions, breathing heavily, frothing at the mouth (tradition has it that he was eplleptic), furiously pursuing those who regarded sex with some detachment or even dared to think of it as a source of pleasure. It has long been my firm opinion that in terms of hypothetical pleasure/pain units, Paul the individual is responsible for more pain caused to the human race over the centuries than any other single person, and that is saying a lot. He is a marvelous poet (cf. Romans especially, Ephesians, Galatians) but unaware of his own limitations."

On the sixth of March 1993, he wrote another short letter: "Having struggled with the problem of religion for so long and so intensely, it is not possible for me to feel any sort of indifference towards those who are seriously struggling with the same problem complex. It took me forty seven years to find an answer that satisfied me as a working basis for metaphysical questions, one that I don't have to modify with every new massacre or paradox or grief."

He continued: "I have a bit of a fear that my two letters in answer to yours have so far contained enough material to confuse you but not enough to meet your minimal needs in the matter of comprehension. So, I'm going to try to deal with a further aspect of the question of religious belief, especially the Plymouth Brethren version, in the hope of giving you enough to enable you to answer your own questions, so to speak, but not so much as to give you the feeling of being the object of a propaganda campaign. So, I want to deal with the aspects of the character of Yahweh, a.k.a., Jehovah."

"As to 'Yahweh,' I prefer this transliteration from the Hebrew because 'Jehovah' is so corrupted by Christian accretions. For example [from a hymn we sang in Meeting]: 'Our love is oft-times low; Our joy still ebbs and flows; But peace with God remains the same; No change Jehovah knows,' – where the tribal God Yahweh is sort of replaced by the interchangeable God/Jehovah pair. I think there is much to be said which isn't part of the traditional portrait."

He also referred to a picture he had sent me of a painting of the Midian children. "You've perhaps already identified the chief characters in the photo I sent you, entitled 'The Midian Children,' which is a portrayal of the events described in Numbers 31, particularly verses 7, 9, and 14-18. If you want to look this up, don't hesitate to read the whole chapter or even the book, but keep your mind open to what is really going on here."

I opened my Bible to Numbers 31 (KJV). Certainly I had read this passage before, because I had read the whole Bible at one time or another, and some parts many times over. But sometimes the olde English, the droning on of the "thees" and "thous," apparently caused my brain to lose its inquisitiveness. "Look at verse 7," he said: "'they slew all the males.' Just like that. Five words, and no honest reader can doubt their meaning." I read on with increasing discomfort. "And of the virgin girls? In verse 18, Moses says: 'keep them alive for yourselves,' but (verse 17) 'kill every woman that hath known man by lying with him.'"

"You may wonder," he continued, "should your habits of treating Old Testament interpretation resemble mine in my former Christian days, why I raise the subject in this context, when great men, for example English Victorians (e.g., Tennyson, Faraday, Victoria herself), swallowed the Mosaic line hook, line and sinker, muttering doubtlessly to themselves what my parents seem to have thought: 'in those days' God used Israel as the instrument of his 'wrath' and got juvenile pleasure through instigating mass rape and slaughter, although for my parents this pleasure wouldn't have been juvenile, it would have been sincere."

He provided another uncomfortable example: "When Elijah won his bet with the priests of Baal that his Jehovah would 'answer by fire,' I Kings 18:24 (KJV), he had no problem deciding what to do: 'Elijah brought them down to the brook Kishon and slew them there' (same chapter, verse 40). Since there were 450 of them, the mechanics of the slaughter aren't immediately obvious, but it isn't all that important: what is immediately obvious is that Yahweh wasn't tolerating any half-way measures when it came to his own place in the various pantheons of that day. About what you'd expect from a sort who spends most of the Old Testament pouting, plotting revenge, repenting himself of the evil, etc."

"One story didn't get past me even as a child," he continued, "but I put it in the 'you'll understand that when you're older' category: the children, 'little' children we are told expressly, (II Kings 2:23-24, KJV) who mocked Elisha on his return from Elijah's ascension, who said something like 'you go up too, baldy, hah hah' – I can just hear it – and he cursed them in the name of Yahweh 'and there came forth two she-bears out of the wood and tare forty and two children of them.' For me, one who is stimulated to love or admiration of so infantile a creature is in a sorry state, to put it mildly. So much for Yahweh, at least for today."

Bud closed this letter by saying: "Now I've written most of what I wanted to say to you in these first three replies to your own letter which moved me so much. You'll realize there's a lot more I could, and on request would say, but the problems are deep and central, and I don't wish to propagate my feelings without knowing whether I'm hurting you. So, let me thank you once again for opening yourself to me, hoping you have accepted the spirit of my replies, and at least perceived where I wanted to go with my words."

9

ON BELIEF

Bud's letters affected me deeply. Here was a close relative who had grown up in the Meeting, in the Plymouth Brethren, in a home environment much like my own. His brother was my father. In turn, their father was a strict fundamentalist, like mine, with little sense of humor. But, unlike my father, Bud seemed to understand me. He accepted my assertion that no subject was taboo and proceeded to test it. He vocalized ideas and thoughts that were violently counter to the religious environment in which I had been inculcated. He criticized the behavior of the government of the country in which we both grew up. Yet, he appeared to know what he believed, and why! He had empathy for my struggle. Clearly, I had a lot to think about.

I had previously sent Bud a quote from William James' essay *The Will to Believe*,[1] wherein he refers to a quote from Fitz-James Stephen and Pascal's wager:

'In all important transactions of life we have to take a leap in the dark.... If we decide to leave the riddles unanswered, that is a choice; if we waver in our answer, that, too, is a choice; but whatever choice we make, we make it at our peril. If a man chooses to turn his back altogether on God and the future, no one can prevent him; no one can show beyond reasonable doubt that he is mistaken. If a man thinks otherwise and acts as he thinks, I do not see that any one can prove that he is mistaken. Each must act as he thinks best; and if he is wrong, so much the worse for him.

We stand on a mountain pass in the midst of whirling snow and blinding mist, through which we get glimpses now and then of paths which may be deceptive. If we stand still we shall be frozen to death. If we take the wrong road we shall be dashed to pieces. We do not certainly know whether there is any right one. What must we do? 'Be strong and of a good courage.' Act for the best, hope for the best, and take what comes.... If death ends all, we cannot meet death better.'

"I know," I said, "this quote sounds like a cop-out, and perhaps it is. Yet it's true that nobody has a monopoly on 'the truth,' although many people, e.g., Pat Robertson and other TV evangelists, behave like they do." – "However," I said, "I also have a quote by Galileo Galilei on my study wall: 'I do not feel obliged to believe that that same God who has endowed us with sense, reason and intellect has intended us to forego their use.'"

At this point, I was still convinced that the Biblical God existed. At the same time, I began to think critically about the foundations of my beliefs. I was challenging the premises and conclusions of my adamant religious upbring-ing. But, not only did I still live my life based on the assump-tion that God existed, I feared Him. I didn't fully enter into the contradiction of fearing the "God of Love." I clung tenaciously to the truths that had been indelibly stamped into my brain. After all, who was I to claim that God didn't exist? Would God strike me down for my skepticism and doubts?

I let Bud's letters marinate in my brain for a few months, and sent a reply in late summer. "I'm simultaneously fascinated and disturbed by your opinions and need time to digest them," I said. "I would characterize my own stance as having long-held questions as to why God allows certain events to occur. I have never seriously questioned God's existence, yet my faith waned, then remained fairly constant, i.e., increasingly I simply didn't care. I was so tired of the same old lines and the same old fright tactics used by the Meeting to keep its flock in line. Thus, I had become somewhat comfortable with a simple personal relationship with God, i.e., I talked to God any time I wanted, and read the Bible whenever I wanted; comfortable and convenient; God on my own terms."

"Yet," I wrote, "I've known that such an arrangement probably wouldn't work forever, and that sooner or later, I'd have to do something with this relationship. Then I wrote to you, curious about what your thoughts were. While I am very happy we are writing, and look forward to your letters, I must admit I'm quite uncomfortable with 'telling God that He doesn't exist.'"

"Today," I continued, "I may believe in God because I want to, and perhaps because I need to emotionally, yet at the inception of my belief as a child, I believed because I *knew* it was *the* 'TRUTH.' My eyes had been opened and I had seen the truth. Non-believers were simply blind. Such a belief is not easy to turn away from even when one has questions that continually loom overhead like storm clouds."

However, "I find your arguments wherein you refer to

passages in the Bible, e.g., Numbers 31, much more disconcerting than your fault-finding with the way people throughout history have behaved. Whether God should interfere or intercede, or not, is His choice. Can we criticize Him for not interfering? Most certainly. Yet, if there is a God, and He is the creator of all that exists, an infinite intelligence, etc., can we claim to have the same perspective He might have?"

"But, I do relate to your difficulty in attempting to fuse the concepts: God is good and God is almighty. The character of God, as self-reported through human instruments (in the Bible), is indeed disturbing, especially the book of Numbers. As you said, He has admitted to running a war and I have difficulty reconciling such accounts with the concept of a loving God, whether the victims are heathen (i.e., as such, they might deserve it) or not."

I also had new questions for him: "Regarding the never-dying soul, you note that we've been poked and prodded by science for years without anything turning up. Would it be possible to test for a soul, given that it cannot be observed? Metaphysics is simply not recognized by science, is it?" Also, "in your recent letter you said: 'Your faith is something you sacrifice your children's moral and intellectual development to, having already sacrificed your own.'" – I asked him to elaborate further.

He responded, first by commenting on the Fitz-James Stephen's quote I had sent him. It "impressed me while I was still a Christian, thus dating my exposure to it as at least forty years ago; [it] rings all the truer today. It certainly doesn't seem a cop-out to me. Like Stephen's man on the mountain pass, we make choices in these matters without adequate information because we *must*. To make no choice is an obvious variety of making a choice (by definition, not by logical development). You can't escape death by suicide."

He continued: "As to the, or a, deity, my views are quite clear: divinities are without exception the handiwork of men or women, a formulation given with unusual precision by the world-famous renal physiologist Homer Smith in the title of his book: *Man and his Gods.*[2] I'm aware that this makes me technically an 'atheist,' and at the practical level I am one, but I dislike the term and don't use it to describe myself. Because to give yourself such a label is to say: there is no God/god/gods, while I say merely: there is no God/god/gods who fits the traditional description of Him specifically omniscient and omnipotent. If he is one he can't be the other. Theologians have racked their brains over this paradox since before recorded history no doubt, and still do so because their emotions call or rather scream for it."

"To me it seems that a problem still without even the vestige or beginning of an answer after millennia is probably wrongly defined, or approached or (as I see it) conceived. Virtually all human races have constructed their gods to comfort them in their troubles, and having been constructed on this basis, they were immediately conscripted (the word is well-chosen, even if I do have to say it myself!) for military service: 'Oh Lord our God, arise; Scatter his (that is, the king's) enemies; And make them fall' and probably much later they were employed, or re-assigned if you prefer, to be omniscient and omnipotent at the same time."

"Now," he continued, "it would seem that being or trying to be both O's at the same time is logically futile because they represent literally, very literally indeed, a contradiction in terms, and not simply a party game. And now I can say why I don't think of myself as an atheist at the theoretical level: because all gods are the work of man, they should not be punished with disbelief for their failure to solve a moral equation which is improperly formulated by human (all too human, as Nietzsche put it) logicians. But at least I am then agnostic, as you might ask."

"No, I'm nothing of the kind when it comes to attributing divinity to creatures of man's poetic fantasies. No ifs, ands or buts about these guys: they are creatures, not divinities and I'm sorry for them, they're operating without a license. And in my bureau, any God/god/gods caught running a war is or are automatically disqualified immediately and forever-more. No punishment considering they were only doing what they were made for but no reinstatement either, considering what they were made for!"

He further commented: "You wonder whether I think I have a 'never-dying soul.' The answer, as will scarcely surprise you, is: no. And that applies to me because I'm a member of a race which has been examined, checked, analyzed and experimented upon like nothing else before or since without anything turning up which (like hypnosis, for example) has more than a threadbare skeleton of an exis-tence and which at the practical level is not so individual-ized as to prevent inductive treatment. By which I'm trying to say that the existence of a soul separate from the body is like that of 'God/god/gods,' especially suspect because the notion serves to comfort and to reassure emotionally, specif-ically being constructed to attenuate the suffering associated with the phenomenon of death. Theories constructed to meet emotional needs are historically long-lived, not because of any element of truth in the hypotheses but because of the long-lived quality inherent in the emotional needs concerned."

He closed by including a post-script: "I fear [the contents

of this letter] may seem to you not only irreverent (that is at least partially intended) but even flippant, and that is by no means intended. But when after decades of fighting my father and, less intensively, much of the rest of my family over their insistence that the bloodthirsty (as I see him) god of the Bible be treated as the Prince of Peace, then my sense of logical and moral outrage is so activated that in writing about it I fear I may not always stop short of a flippancy which is, well, inappropriate. But I'm convinced that anyone who could write as you have done has been through enough self-testing to provide himself with personalized criteria stable enough to prevent confusion when confronting opinions heretofore heard only from ideological opponents. So if I don't get a 'cease and desist' order from you I plan to go further."

Well, despite feeling confused and even offended by some of what Bud had written, I wasn't going to ask him to stop. He was the first family member who didn't immediately reject my questions and doubts outright as blasphemous. Unlike my father, he didn't condemn me for doubting. And although I was uncomfortable with some of his writings, I knew at least he was being honest. And so our letters continued to cross the Atlantic.

10

GODS AND HUMAN SUFFERING

I n his next letter, Bud wrote "I want to take up the question of human suffering and the God/god/gods problem. Henry D. Thoreau once wrote 'the mass of men lead lives of quiet desperation.' I remember first encountering this observation at fifteen or sixteen, and giving myself the Plymouth Brethren's standard explanation of 'sin!' for everything less than ideal. So it was that I kept [this explanation] warm in memory during the years of struggle until I was ready for John Fowles's synthesis in *The Aristos*[1] and Bertrand Russell's [writings]. Thanks mostly to the teachings of these two gentlemen I developed the habit of looking at paradoxes directly, and with more concentration. – I've never encountered any attempt to deny, let alone refute Thoreau's observation (although I've little doubt that attempts have been made by those I call 'Wheaton professors,' i.e., learned men who've sold their rights to intellectual probity for Esau's 'mess of pottage,' Genesis 25: 29-34). Therefore, I assume it is seen by most others as I do: irrefutable. Even if some savant tries to explain, like Leibniz that 'everything is for the best in the best of all possible worlds' (not Leibniz's phrase, but his thought formulated by Voltaire for the mouth of his Leibniz-impersonator, Dr. Pangloss, in *Candide*[2]) he will be treated at best as eccentric."

"Now what can we, must we, say about a race and its God/god/gods which lead lives of quiet desperation? At least, I should think, that something here went wrong, very wrong, way back when things were getting started, stayed on the wrong track, and now has atomic and hydrogen bombs, to mention only two of the results of centuries of suffering, freshly and continuously available for our delectation."

"And what depth and breadth of suffering! The very notion of personal freedom is to my knowledge relatively modern, not truly older than 18th-century France. 'Enlightened' Greeks of the ancient world had an economy which depended on slaves for all except the more exalted positions, and those holding these had a private retinue of slaves to run their households. As recently as Napoleon-Europe war was regarded as normal, and the only people who objected to Bismarck's war of 1870-1871 were the French, who lost it. In history wherever we look we see plagues and pestilence, starvation and slaughter, all this regarded as normal, if you please. During the 'Thirty Years' War' (1618-1648) when Protestant armies from the north fought Catholic armies from the south (to simplify the story extremely) the one thing (apart from killing each other) that both sides did freely was to kill peasants, mainly for fun, as best I can judge, and livestock (for fun and food). It was Bosnia ∧ 10 or 100."

"Until modern times it was normal for a woman whose baby was in the 'breech' position to die in childbirth. During my youth it was normal to die of 'pneumonia' (until the arrival of penicillin in the early 1940s, pneumococcal pneumonia was known as 'the old man's friend') and diphtheria and syphilis. Imagine a farm family anywhere in the, say, ninth century. They live in tents or huts, no heating except from their own bodies and those of domestic animals (cows and sheep). People older than thirty have lost their teeth and depend on soup. The few older than forty five-to-fifty can't see well, if only because of presbyopia, couldn't read even when they could see. No distinguishing between fact and fancy, the Bible tells us 'though shalt not suffer a witch to live' (Exodus 22:18, KJV) without telling us how to identify one, an omission directly responsible for the deaths of thousands of elderly women in the late Middle Ages, angels and demons everywhere. I suppose that more than 90% of the human lives which have been lived and are being lived are considerably inferior in quality to the average dog's life. You won't easily persuade me that humanity is the creation of an all-knowing, all-powerful, all-loving God/god/gods!"

"So there we have almost four full pages" he concluded, "and I'll let it go at that for today. There is something so emotionally rewarding in the experience of being free to express myself openly to close family members that I tend to run off at the mouth. Now let me wish you, Dan, a good end-of-semester and peace of mind and good fortune in making and carrying out plans for whatever comes next."

11

MAGIC THINKING

Each time I went to the mailbox and found a letter from Bud, chills went up my spine. His writings inspired, challenged and excited me like little else. And being in the midst of my graduate studies, I needed intellectual diversions. But my studies converged with the contents of Bud's letters as I studied research methods, mathematics, the scientific process, the role of theory, hypotheses and so on. As a result, I began to distinguish more carefully between belief and reality.

However, the ideas he was conveying simultaneously scared me and caused me internal turmoil. The contents of his arguments were poles apart from what I'd been taught. Yet he had also been brought up in an environment similar to mine, where doubt was sin. He understood the mindsets and beliefs that my father and his father represented, along with their mental traps and moral pitfalls. Thus, I respected the path he had taken to reach a world-view that explained the pain and suffering in the world we both perceived. However, I still clung to what I called the middle-of-the-road approach, where my belief in a God who loved and cared for me remained intact, but where strict adherence to biblical rules and fear of a vengeful sin-hating God were absent. I wanted the love and care, but not the fear and intolerance. Thus, I needed to see my own way forward through the fog.

Bud began his next letter by saying he would address some loose ends left over from the entries on religion in his previous letters. But "first, I'd like to thank you for the spirit of sincere concern and inquiry which came through and between the lines especially of your last letter. I've answered without trying to suppress a certain irreverence of spirit which always rises in me when I think of my first childish, then youthful efforts to fuse the concepts: God is good and God is almighty and ending in hopeless futility. My present views you know already, and I can assure you of my respect for your position, even though I do believe you will have to give it up over the years, unless you decide you want peace and give up questioning, a measure which for me equals intellectual and spiritual and moral death." – Damn! I remember when I first read this sentence, then reread it, at first offended, then thoughtful, then re-considering, and ultimately wholly agreeing with it.

He continued, "It would never do to agree with something I say just because I said it, but a procedure all too common among believers in any specialized subject. I get the feeling that you aren't in very much danger of this particular trap, otherwise I'd never have felt free to give my firm opinions as openly as I did and will do."

So, "let me then return to a subject I raised, and then dropped, in my first letter of this recent series: that of 'middle-of-the-roadism' in religion. In religion we deal with claims which are necessarily exclusive in character because we are dealing with charismatic treatment of subjects which cannot, in their very essence, be treated objectively (scientifically, if you will). Hence the enormous importance in all religions of 'faith.' Yes, your faith is something you sacrifice your children's moral and intellectual development to, having already sacrificed your own, and the passion is the same whether you're giving them Dianetics or Mormonism (on re-reading: is it pure chance I picked two of the money-hungriest organizations on the 'religious' scene?). The common feature is the dependence on emotions, the rejection of the objective in all forms as a matter of principle, the acceptance of magic thinking."

"I have little doubt that magic thinking arose along with the birth of thought and thinking itself. At least the oldest of old religions (Egypt, Babylon, Peru, Mexico, India, etc.) come to us with a full-blown panoply of gods and goddesses requiring what is known to Christianity as 'propitiatory' behavior designed to appease 'the wrath of a sin-hating God' ('the Savior's obedience and blood, Hide all our transgressions from view' – ouch!). But it is the absolutist aspect of each charismatic religion which to my way of thinking damns any attempt at finding a middle-of-the-road position which is acceptable to all parties. It is qualitatively similar, to use a topical example, to drawing a map of the territories which previously constituted Yugoslavia to which all the warring factions agree. The paradox is not supplied from outside, but rather is inherent in the exclusive nature of the conflicting claims."

"So, if you find yourself warming to my arguments, I shall be pleased but even more concerned that you swallow nothing unchewed. For it will be evident to you already, even if you haven't chanced to formulate it for yourself in this way, that my rejection of magic thinking is basic, is fundamental, because it contravenes the all-or-none claims of charismatic religion which have thereby made a holistic formulation of the basis of the controversy. If you've never given the concept of 'magic thinking' much thought, I propose you do so because I think scales will fall from your eyes."

"Should the clay say to the potter: 'why hast thou made me thus?' Indeed it should, in my view, what's more it should hold its tongue until it has received a satisfactory answer. If a pot has the gift of speech it should refrain from using it, though, until it has checked to see whether it has a brain too, for without the latter the benefits to the environment are dubious at best. Bertrand Russell was once asked what he would do should he die and find himself, contrary to his expectations, in the presence of the White-bearded One. He replied: 'I should ask Him why he made it so impossible to believe in Him for those on earth.' This is the spirit I like. It is altogether proper, as I see it, to hold God to the standards of intellectual and emotional honesty which we use in dealing with our fellow men, and radicals like me would even go so far as to require of Him 100% honesty, a stupefying but in my judgment altogether appropriate demand."

"You say (I'll summarize) you like to have a God to whom you can confess weaknesses, malfeasances even, someone with whom you can cultivate an essentially 'chummy' relationship. I think this is one of the most profound of human desires, shared by everyone whose feelings are sensitive enough to be worthy of consideration. But again, I feel this is a variety of the 'if wishes were horses, then beggars might ride' phenomenon. I believe most feeling people wish the same, but to go to the extreme of hiring the first available deity, in this case Yahweh, with his established defects of character, seems a bit radical."

Looking back, I admit to having, just as Bud described, a chummy relationship with an entity I had been raised to simultaneously love and fear. But that relationship proved to be malleable and morphed over time to one that was affected by my personal, daily observations of the pain and suffering so evident in the world.

12

SCIENCE, TRUTH AND FAITH

I received another letter from Bud in late summer 1993. "Your letter received three days ago moved me deeply, more than I can recall having been moved by a letter in recent years. I recognize above all the obvious sincerity which guides both choice of themes and of comment. And I honor you for trusting me enough to express thoughts which while necessary to give shape and substance are surely unspeakable, and that in the most literal sense of the term, in (for example) your parental home."

So, "I've decided to start with 'science,' since experience has taught me that with the exception of its rival, what you call 'metaphysics,' no subject of overweening importance is so loaded with misunderstanding and confusion, both honest and dishonest. The subject is so important because the basic concept of epistemology (the study of knowledge, i.e., how we can know what is true or untrue, and why) is directly influenced."

"I'm not going to write a textbook of epistemology, but rather sketch out a few principles which have come to seem critical to me. – I'd like to start by saying: science is the daughter of technology, the codification and symbolic formulation of 'truths,' i.e., concepts which lead to construction of recipes (whether for caramel pudding or a suspension bridge) which reflect the 'true' nature of things. And that in such a way that one familiar with the ('scientific') principles behind the recipe can reproduce the pudding or bridge or what-have-you at a distance, and without having to consult the author of the report. 'Reproducibility' is the key word here: if a person reports that they have created this or that with these or those properties or qualities and nine out of ten of those who attempt to repeat this work succeed, this report qualifies as worthy of belief, at least until someone proves the opposite. Proving the opposite may turn out to be the service of the tenth investigator who didn't confirm the original report. It may even be that the new findings resulting from the attempt to explain the discrepancy are far more useful, both in theory and practice, than the findings which led to their study in the first place. And now the essence: what have I been trying to say? Just this: 'science' is interested in 'truth' as manifested by reproducibility."

He continued: "There is a sense in science that whatever always occurs, given specified initial conditions are the same, is in some (perhaps ineffable) sense, true. Such 'trueness,' if I may coin a word, is never absolute, for the best products of man's mind are usually modified by new discoveries. And now I think we are in a position to distinguish between science and metaphysics, to deal with the core of the matter. It is characteristic, basic, essential, fundamental (you get the direction) to science to remain forever incomplete, to seek criticism of every result and still more of generalizations or rules or laws. This, I hope also answers your question: 'metaphysics is simply not recognized by science is it?' The answer, of course, is that metaphysics is recognized by science, but not as a discipline whose results can everywhere, anywhere be reproduced by anyone who understands the basic principles. Where would we be if every idiotic pronouncement of Billy Graham's or Pat Robertson's were given the same credibility as the work of some self-critical scientist playing by known rules?"

"The story of Albert Einstein illustrates some of these aspects dramatically. He was born in 1879 and published his theory of special relativity at twenty six, in 1905, demolishing, among other things the concept of the 'luminiferous (i.e., light-bearing) ether.' His crowning work, the general theory of relativity, came eleven years later, in 1916, when he was thirty seven. Quantum mechanics, in its basic form, was discovered in 1925-1926, by a German, a Dane and an Austrian. Then as now one of its central features is the 'uncertainty principle,' which introduces a modified concept, among other things, of causality. Einstein didn't care for that at all and spent the rest of his life fighting the new theory on purely emotional terms, searching for a major new unifying hypothesis which forever eluded his grasp. I've gone into detail about this story to show that there is no such thing as 'science' in the sense of a monolithic entity dispensing approval and disapproval. What counts in science is reproducibility at the practical level and flexibility at the theoretical."

"As to faith, this is a subject which is so personal that I feel hesitant to take it up, at least by mail. I will point out, though, that my adherence to the 'scientific' viewpoint is, in virtually every important respect I can think of, as much a faith as any borne by those whose orientation is primarily of the religious sort."

· · ·

BUD HAD EARLIER NOTED that "you and I were taught to believe (have faith in) things because they were so described in a given source, the Bible, not because they were or are true." – Unfortunately, the situation hasn't changed much in my family. My father quite recently, in 2023, shouted at me over the phone: "I believe the Bible!" He sounded a bit hysterical, almost in a panic, and it occurred after he told me in direct, haughty terms that he would never solicit advice from me because of my beliefs, or lack thereof. This, despite the fact that he's never asked what I believe. It reminded me of Bud's previous assessment of this attitude: "My mind is made up; don't confuse me with facts!"

Bud finished this letter by saying, "There is one matter I wish to take up before I hit the end of this page, and that is your question: how do I approach life given my point of view? I can only answer from the depths of my heart: much, much better than before I acquired it. The book by John Fowles, *The Aristos*,[1] describes reality in the way I now sense it, and I find his approach both reasonable and comforting. It is so obvious to me, in hindsight, that God/god/gods is a product of human brains and not the reverse, that I leave the matter alone. There are very few people who care anything about these matters and those who do are quite content with a church visit at Easter or Christmas, or for the adventurous, both! Yet most of them behave properly, even laudably, most of the time, enough to keep society functioning at some level."

13

MAGIC THINKING AND EXPLOITATION

I n Bud's next letter, he wrote, "While growing up, I became increasingly convinced that my parents were not only truly ignorant, they were proud of being so, and over the years it became evident that no bridges could be built across such a canyon."

So, "I'd like to spare you some of the dead-ends I had to check out individually and thus have the chance of getting the feeling that someone else in the category of seeker might benefit from my scars without himself having to suffer from the same preceding wounds. Am I trying to convert you to my own personal creed? I should hope not, because (for one thing) it is tailored for me, somewhat like a set of dentures which is not suited to communal use. But the principles behind good denture-making are the same and I would not be ashamed if on that basis we found some important points of agreement. I'm not going to search for them, mind you, just welcome them should they appear."

"As I believe I told you, I was considerably older (forty seven) than you are now when I finally realized that an unrecognized addiction to magic thinking left over from my parents' tutelage lay behind my greatest difficulties, and I've been working on that ever since. This aberration isn't surprising when you consider that the Bible from beginning to end is founded on magic thinking, and the different epochs (and authors) merely reflect the current local superstitions of their time and place. The existence (and easy recognizability) of witches was so self-evident to the ancient Jews that they accepted and practiced death sentences on old women who had become a bit senile without finding it legally necessary to describe the crime in a judicial way even for consistency among various tribes."

He continued, "You say that Christians don't challenge God's ways, and I can see what you mean. But this circumstance makes it all the more important, it seems to me, to check and recheck the credentials of the prophets and apostles who claim to be distributing His Word. I must confess that this habit of mine has only convinced me that the God of the Bible is, as I've mentioned before, the product of man's imagination, and if that seems to call for trying out the other gods, they don't come out recognizably better. It seems that a just god or God is a contradiction in terms; indeed that is my own conviction."

"Speaking of my own convictions, I think a rather serious misinterpretation resulted from my attempt to describe the basis of the system of practical ethics which I have constructed, for lack of anything better, for my own use. I certainly didn't mean to imply, much less state, that one 'ought not to do harm.'" For example, "you harm the atmosphere every time you exhale by shifting the atmospheric ratio O_2/CO_2 slightly in the wrong direction. Every defecation is a catastrophe for hundreds of thousands of E. coli bacilli, most of whom don't survive separation from the warm (37 C), dark, wet environment into which they were born."

"I can't remember how I formulated my rule for our use, but it consists of taking a negative attitude towards exploitation, particularly the exploitation of our fellow man. This is a rather radical approach, something I failed to realize when it came to me, for exploitation is one of the comparatively few evils which is fostered, promulgated and cultivated in every human society which has come to my notice."

"Slavery," he noted, "crops up in history wherever and whenever we look. The social order of the ancient Greeks, which at the time of Pericles and Socrates we so much admire, was based on slavery, and that of a sort which didn't foster the production of slave children. The result: when slaves died out it was necessary to replace them by the means which led to their existence (as slaves) in the first place: war. For the klines on which Socrates and Plato and the rest reclined to dine, were prepared – and the dishes washed and the floor mopped, and the children put to bed – by slaves who were simply prisoners of war, virtually none of which had any hope of freedom ever. What surprised me when I learned this is that these wars of exploitation often had procurement of prisoners to function as slaves as primary motivations. – Today the [great manufacturers] 'lay off' thousands of employees when times are bad, as they are now. Any General Director of one of these companies could write a book on exploitation over a weekend, I imagine."

"The exploitation of children by parents is another neglected aspect of this problem, which I won't go into today. – When, as in third world countries, it is often economically unavoidable, it is perceived as such and at least regretted. But what about 'first world' children who are brought up in such a way that their minds, yes, I'm thinking of myself among others, are permanently deformed and such attempts at restoration, as are or can be made, show at best a trivial success, since you can't restore what was never permitted to undergo normal development in the first place."

14

ANTI MIDDLE-OF-THE-ROADISM

"My urge to put thoughts on paper for you is unabated," Bud wrote in his next letter, "so today I'm going to try to touch a few more bases in the hope what comes will carry sincerity, even if I come across increasingly like an old windbag."

"You may be wondering why I keep coming back to themes which you may suppose I had already covered adequately, at least for you. The short answer is that I wish to take advantage (without exploiting!) of your willingness to listen to me, unique in my family, and I want to argue as powerfully as I possibility can against the middle-of-the road position which you have chosen to defend, even in matters of religion and faith."

"I've given you, in previous letters, my arguments against, for example, middle-of-the-roadism in religious matters. I know no subject which can even be compared with religion for the complexity and extent of emotions which it calls forth. People love, 'for God and country,' to go to war (it was Jews who screamed 'Saul hath slain his thousands, but David his ten thousands' (I Samuel 18:7, KJV)) and

Christians who make their own bouillabaisse of the various ingredients in such formulations as: 'Christ the Royal Master; Leads against the foe; Forward into battle; See His armies go.' In my experience the ratio of militancy to fanaticism among religious people is close to one-to-one."

"Perhaps you will object that this justifies, if anything, your attempt to defend a middle position. My counter would be: there is, there can be logically, no middle position in fields of human experience which evoke fanatical beliefs with tendencies toward violence. Jesus got it clear in his laconic observation: 'he that is not with me is against me' (Matthew 12:30, KJV). I've never encountered a convincing commentary on those occasions where Jesus himself is described as behaving hysterically: 'Ye serpents, ye generation of vipers, how can ye escape the damnation of hell?' (Matthew 23:33, KJV). The Pharisees who were the objects of this vituperation seem to have been quite ordinary citizens whose 'crimes' ('ye compass land and sea to make one proselyte, and when he is found, ye make him two-fold more the child of hell than yourselves' (Matthew 23:15, KJV)) are of the sort that would be handled in the modern judiciary by the civil and not the criminal courts, cheating widows and orphans of their inheritance(s), for example."

"THIS SEEMS suitable a place as any other to comment on another aspect of this problem complex which has, sooner or later, to be confronted in any analysis of charismatic religions. I call it anti-intellectualism. Since the very existence of charismatic religion is due to charismatic founders (whether Moses or Brigham Young isn't all that important) whose position is always challenged by those adherents whose charismatic gifts and talents have a different source than those of the founders, it is in the interests of the founders to avoid intelligent discussion or indeed any discussion, since that sort of thing tends, to put it mildly, to promote skepticism."

"In my experience this anti-intellectualism among fundamentalist Christians often takes the form of glorification of ignorance: 'Oh Savior, whom absent we love; Whom not having seen we adore;' [and] 'Though the shore we hope to land on, only by report is known; Yet we freely all abandon, led by that report alone' are two examples [from hymns we used to sing] that come to mind. Anti-intellectualism is reflected in the Roman Catholic usage, in which believers are encouraged not to study the Bible because only clergymen can interpret it. Glorification of ignorance in the Catholic church is differentiated [although this has changed somewhat]: the laity is kept ignorant as far as possible, and that is almost infinitely possible since most people instinctively prefer ignorance to knowledge."

"The main reason for this is that knowledge is inherently inimical to prejudices, and for most people their prejudices are essential to their sanity. And this is not a pseudo-literary description but hard cold fact. That, in my opinion, and nothing else, explains why war is almost more 'normal' for most of our race today and in history than ever peace is or has been. But I must now admit that going on would mean a new sheet. No, not today!"

15

RESPONDING TO BUD REGARDING DISHONESTY

My letters to Bud were in a ratio of approximately one to three. But I finally answered him in January 1994.

"I must admit I finally see your conflict between an omniscient, omnipotent and loving God. For years I've questioned (to myself) how God could be 'love,' and 'unwilling that any should perish' (II Peter 3:9, KJV), and yet have 'chosen in Him (certain people, like me!) before the foundation of the world,' (Ephesians 1:4, KJV) and also be no 'respecter of persons' (Acts 10:34, KJV)." – In essence, I was asking why should God take me to heaven, while sending somebody else to hell, especially if the hell-bound person hadn't done anything overtly wrong except for not believing in Him?

I continued ... "At times I have thought that an all-knowing God surely knew Adam and Eve would eat the fruit of the tree and that the curse of man's sin would result in consequences predetermined by Himself. So, much like creating rules for a board game one has invented, God invented the rules by which his creatures would have to play, all the while knowing what the outcome would be: People sent to a God-created hell for not believing in Him."

"I like your reference, in your earlier letter, to Bertrand Russell, where he said that he would like to ask God, if he met up with Him in the afterlife, why He didn't make it easier for people to believe in Him. So, I find it increasingly difficult to believe in the God of the Bible, yet resist believing that there is no Supreme Being, i.e., that there was no creation, etc."

"I now find it frighteningly easy to switch from one perspective to the other, one moment thinking in the way I was taught as a child, and the next, seeing an incongruity in my thoughts or in life, that there simply cannot be a God, else 'things wouldn't be the way they are.' This, as you can well imagine, is an uncomfortable state of affairs that I don't believe will be rectified any time soon. For now I can only say that I would like to believe in God, and sometimes I do."

"I liked your discussion of science and 'how we know what is true or untrue.' You say that 'science is interested in truth as manifested by reproducibility.' I agree, yet science has limitations, i.e., if there are spirits, angels, and so forth, science has no means by which to detect them. And if man is indwelt by the Holy Ghost, science hasn't detected that either. Further, men like my father, would tell you that they have felt the Lord's guidance, care, watchful eye, and so on, and wholeheartedly believe it. Is this 'feeling' anything that can be tested scientifically?"

I continued, "Science relegates 'miracles,' and the like, to random events and unexplainable phenomena, because they cannot be tested empirically, let alone reproduced or the results generalized to other places or populations. So, as much as I like the pureness of good, unbiased science, and its 'fail-to-disprove' approach, I believe it is limited by man and his tools and technology (we really are sort of a helpless bunch)."

"Your concept of magic thinking has, as you proposed in an earlier letter, struck me as similar to 'scales falling from my eyes.' For me it is so intuitively appealing, and at the same time it's something that I almost wish I'd never heard given that I honestly would like to believe in God. But I must agree with your statement that 'the Bible from beginning to end is founded on magic thinking.'"

Bud had been right in this regard. Scales had fallen from my eyes. I began to see the so-called miracles described in the Bible through the lens of magic thinking and myth. Jesus walking on water, the creation of the earth and Adam and Eve, the talking snake, the instant development of many languages at Babel, Lot's wife turning into a pillar of salt, the plagues in Egypt, Moses and his burning bush, the manna that magically appeared to feed the Israelites, the collapse of the walls of Jericho, Balaam's talking donkey, the list is nearly endless. And how could I forget, the virgin birth!

I continued, "I like your idea of 'checking the credentials of the prophets and apostles who claim to be distributing His Word.' This is a logical approach given the reporting of unpalatable events like the slaying of the Midian children you referred to in Numbers, Chapter 31. – I'm amazed that I have believed the Bible on its own word alone. I certainly have not asked enough questions; but as you (wrote), questions were discouraged in the Meeting, to which I would add: decrees were made!"

"IN YOUR LAST LETTER, I must say you were pretty rough on Aunt Fran and your Dad, portraying their position as 'I'm right, therefore I needn't be honest.'" [Aunt Fran was entering our discussion because she was very adamant in her beliefs and passive-aggressive in expressing them to family members, much like my grandfather Harold.] Do you honestly believe that they didn't unequivocally believe what they said to you about Christ? – I believe we have corresponded enough that I can tell you a little story about my childhood. Most of my first sixteen years were spent on Maple Drive where we lived next door to 'Mr. and Mrs. Wright.' It wasn't until I was nearly thirty years old that I discovered that the old couple weren't Mr. and Mrs., i.e., they weren't married! When I found out, I was completely dumbfounded and pissed off. Mom said, 'didn't you ever pick up on the way I called them Mr. Wright and Ethel?' Today I sort of chuckle about it, yet it appears that my parents were so insecure in their beliefs, and unwilling to advise their children of the real state of affairs, that the couple was living together unmarried, 'in sin,' that they side-stepped the situation. You could also say they lied by omission."

"I sometimes look back on my childhood and wonder how I could have been so naive. I can only say that, although (my parents) aren't without faults, they certainly are not hypocritical. They truly live the way they believe. I marveled the day, when I was about 8, when I saw my Dad's thumb take a direct and vicious hit from a hammer he was swinging and all he said was 'OUCH!' I also never saw my father take a drink of alcohol except the wine he supped on Sunday during Breaking of Bread. I've never heard him swear, never! I've also seen him refrain from buying stock in IBM, even when it was easy because he considered it an 'unequal yoke' with unbelievers (II Corinthians 6:14, KJV)."

On re-reading these old letters, I recall proposing to my father when I was in my teens, that we were a Christian family only because Christianity was the predominant belief in the USA. Further, that if I had been born in another family in a country that was, say, Muslim, that we would be Muslims. His response, nearly shouted: "you should get down on your knees and thank God for being brought up in the Truth!"

"My point," I continued to Bud, "is that I think I believed what (my parents) said because their lives paralleled their beliefs. They were doing what they KNEW to be RIGHT. – Yes, I have some hard feelings about the way I grew up, and I have sat in a counselor's office for quite a few hours over the years talking about it, but it's history."

"Toward the end of your letter you state 'in my experience anti-intellectualism among fundamentalist Christians often takes the form of glorification of ignorance.' I must agree. And so I long ago backed away from my father's position because I viewed it as impossible and impractical for me to follow in today's complex world and because I viewed it as an 'unhealthy' and unbalanced approach to life. My attitude has always been that if God gave us the ability to see in color and gave us taste-buds, He must want us to enjoy life a little, instead of playing a 'pilgrim in the wilderness' role."

16

SINCERITY, SCIENCE AND MAGIC

B ud's reply to my letter came two weeks later. "I want to lose no time," he said, "in correcting the impression I have apparently given you that I doubt the sincerity of your parents, my father, or Aunt Fran. I'm terribly sorry but I'm going to stick with my depiction of the way their thought comes across to me. Each of them has repeatedly damned my views, or rather what they take to be my views since neither of them has asked me about them."

"They are content to curse me for views of which they know not, and the formula is simple: he obviously doesn't believe what or as I do, therefore he is 1) wrong, and 2) requires reproof and correction. Aunt Fran once wrote me to the effect: 'OK, you won't take it from me but what about the Blessed Lord?' The implication is clear: 'there is such a THING as truth, which can be assessed and measured and weighed and analyzed, and she has got it and if I won't take her word on the results she'll just have to send me elsewhere, apparently preferably to the Source Himself.' This is what I mean by the accusation, which I stick with: 'they are right therefore they needn't be honest.'"

"I don't and never have doubted Aunt Fran's or Harold's sincerity, but I never doubted the sincerity of Hitler or Stalin either and don't have any reason to doubt the sincerity of the various political radicals, such as the Neo-Nazis now starting to try to turn the clock back. So I suspect that what you mean by sincerity may be something to do with absence of fraudulent motives of the kind we must take for granted in the case of the dead dictators and their all-too-lively would-be followers. I don't believe that sincerity in belief has anything whatever to do with the truth or falsehood of the belief, considered objectively."

"And now, having gotten this far, I'd like to ... deal at least in passing with the theme: science. It is not only true, as you point out, that there are things (you mention spirits, angels, the Holy Ghost, etc.) which science cannot even analyze, much less judge and criticize. It is this self-limitation of science, in my judgment, which alone gives it the right to say *anything* about matters which can be analyzed objectively. The Popper criterion of 'falsifiability' (which on linguistic, not conceptual grounds I call 'refutability') may be applied according to the formula: you can only prove what you can disprove. There is *no way* I, or anyone else, could ever disprove the existence of, say, angels. Therefore science is silent on the subject, not out of disinterest, but by the self-discipline which defines its own metier."

A week later, Bud followed up with another reply. "I'm still glowing from your letter, and am prepared to go as far as to say that in view of what you say about magic thinking, the rest of the material is secondary. For if you agree that the Bible is *founded* on magic thinking, as I'm convinced it is, then any exegesis which doesn't take that into consideration is unacceptable in principle. It is immediately evident that prayer of the sort we were raised upon is nothing more than (and nothing less at the same time) a request to the alleged creator of the universe to suspend the laws of physics at least temporarily for the purpose of giving aid and/or assistance and/or comfort to one of the individuals who owes his existence and his desires themselves to those selfsame laws."

He continued, "Jesus walked and talked in a world of magic, responding with reproof when the disciples ('ye of little faith') showed astonishment that a couple of loaves of bread and a few fishes sufficed to still the hunger of several thousand people, or saw him come to them across the water, walking on top of it (as a boy these things confused me – I didn't see why, if he could do *anything*, he didn't simply snap his fingers, so to say, and transpose himself into the boat and save himself the walk – 'You mustn't *ask* such questions,' said my mother). I comforted myself with the thought that at least his walking on the water shored up the (often) weak faith of the disciples. But the whole is pure magic."

"The only other book (among those I've read, of course) which achieves this density of magic as the basis of thought is Bunyun's book, *Pilgrim's Progress*.[1] Here *everything* is symbolic, if not of something else, then of itself. I'm sure we'll be coming back regularly to this theme, if only to check co-ordinates, so to speak."

17

INTELLECTUAL (DIS)HONESTY
REVISITED

Bud and I continued to disagree about his accusation of his father's and aunt's intellectual honesty. My father could easily have been included as an additional perpetrator, but was left out of the primary discussion because of his immediate proximity to both me and Bud. However, I've included this extended discussion because at the present time (2025) in the USA, there are many Christian fundamentalists who are working to force their beliefs and strict rules for living on other people. Thus, the question of whether or not they are intellectually honest is important to address.

Bud's position was this: "The two people most vigorous in their pursuit of force or bamboozling as tools to justify and then enforce the use of pressure to achieve 'harmony' and 'conformity' in my life were my father and my Aunt Fran. Their positions, in my considered judgment, can be summarized in the formula: 'I'm right, therefore I needn't be honest.' This is a pretty grave accusation, but it is the product of many decades of intense reflection, and even if you strongly disagree I stick with it. By now I hope you will have seen what I'm trying to get at. No, I wouldn't change your opinions even if I could do so by just snapping my fingers; but I would like to see you change your own opinions on the basis of a reassessment of your own premises."

In a previous letter I had written: "In your last letter, I must say that you are pretty rough on Aunt Fran and your Dad, re: 'I'm right, therefore I needn't be honest.' Do you honestly believe that they, especially Aunt Fran, didn't unequivocally believe what they said to you about Christ?" I told him of my encounters with Bible preachers, or screechers as I called them, on Cady Mall on the main campus of Arizona State University, who would verbally accost passersby with shouted questions such as 'where will you go when you die?' One day, I was confronted by a screecher with the same question. 'Six feet under!' was my reply to which came the retort: 'you can't, it's either heaven or hell!' I continued my walk without further comment, but the parallel between the Cady Mall Bible cowboys and Bud's father, my grandfather, and Aunt Fran seemed appropriate. "These people," I said, "believe they are licensed by the 'God of the Universe' as monopolists in the truth market, which yields the arrogance you describe in Aunt Fran and Harold."

"Yet," I continued, "from watching my father over the years ... there is an attitude of invincibility one gains from believing they hold a monopoly on *the* Truth that fosters an arrogance and gives the one-on-which-the-truth-is-bestowed a responsibility to spread the truth and yield no ground because non-believers are lost souls bound for hell. Further, when the people they judge to be 'ignorant, uninformed, and/or misled' are family members, the 'truth-holders' act with even more urgency because the family must be together in eternal bliss. I believe Aunt Fran made her arguments to you completely unaware of her magical-thinking-blinders, i.e., that somebody else could hold an 'alternative Truth' and believe it as sincerely as she. It simply wasn't within the realm of possibility since she was in communion with God ('I am the truth' John 14:6, KJV)."

I further characterized my father's position in my own words as: "'I'm right, therefore I needn't consider your objections too seriously since I'm secure in God's truth.' – They believe they hold a monopoly on the truth; and I use the word in its most literal sense, i.e., God-given exclusive possession."

"Perhaps," I continued, "my problem is with your use of the word 'dishonest.' My dictionary defines dishonest as 'disposed to lie, cheat, defraud, or deceive.' All along I have included in my own definition the notion of intent, i.e., that if Aunt Fran was dishonest, she consciously chose to be. In a recent conversation with my father, when I tentatively revealed a few of my doubts about Old Testament veracity, (e.g., that women were judged unclean during menstruation, and that Lot offered his virgin daughters, who he later humped, up to the men of Sodom so that God's scouts could leave in the morning unmolested), he said that unlike me ... he was content to 'leave these things with the Lord, knowing that someday all will be revealed.'"

"However," I continued, "you note that your charge is 'lack of concern for truth because of self-imposed ignorance.' This is a phrase I can both work with and agree. For me it implies no intent to deceive their fellow man. Instead, it speaks, for me, to a separation of knowledge to that of God's versus man's. I'm quite sure that my father or Aunt Fran would state that there are passages in the Bible that appear to be discrepancies, but if we were omniscient, like God, all these apparent discrepancies would disappear."

"I read your words, 'self-imposed ignorance' as referring

to the willing subjugation of all thought to God's Word, safe in the knowledge that 'God said it, I believe it, and that finishes it.' Is this dishonest? Not from the Christian's perspective. And only marginally so from mine, since I can almost feel their conviction, which means that if men disagree, or even have evidence contrary to God's Word, they must be wrong."

In a subsequent letter, Bud sought to further clarify his position: "I used the term 'dishonest' to refer to their basic attitudes, and I remain convinced that in their specific cases, at least, this characterization is both appropriate and necessary."

He continued: "What my father and Aunt Fran and, I greatly fear, many of their 'brothers and sisters in Christ' have in common, and what I meant with the phrase which offended you – 'they are right, therefore they needn't be honest' – is that they both have a private system of beliefs which in each case is not open to discussion yet constantly and thoughtlessly employed to condemn anyone whose views deviate even a little from theirs. – There is a difference though! Aunt Fran in my judgment is truly arrogant, and unaware of being ignorant, whereas my dad is more like a desperado with one gun which he prefers not to use. He senses that his position 'I'm always right' isn't easy to convince others of. But anyone who challenges it, like me as a boy (originally innocently) or youth (innocent no longer) will find out in no uncertain terms what he has done. Neither Aunt Fran nor my father, in my judgment, understands the role of 'fear and trembling' as recommended by Peter" [Philippians 2:12].

Further, he said, "I didn't intend to impugn their characters in the sense that if I gave them a small sum of money to redeem, say, a foreign package at the post office they would keep the change for themselves. No, it is intellectual dishonesty I'm laying to their charge. Subornation to suppression of truth, persecution of people who sincerely disagree with them and have the misfortune of falling into gravitational spheres where they regard their own interpretations as complete, perfect and immune to criticism. I use the phrase 'character deformed by religion' for such people, and include myself when the exposure to such false doctrines as theirs is forced on small children who lack any tools, intellectual or otherwise, to use in self-defense."

In still another letter, he noted: "As you (correctly, as I see it) surmise, Aunt Fran substitutes emotional sincerity for what I call 'intellectual honesty,' and the substitution does her ill. I've had many a conversation with her, and she rigorously avoided anything that might have been interpreted or misinterpreted as preaching, contenting herself with sighs and eyes-heavenward gesticulations which are her trademark. But once back home she composed letters which were, like ex cathedra pronouncements by the pope, open to no discussion, usually ending in some version of one phrase with capital letters and curlicue multiple underlinings and shaded multiple exclamation points, etc.: 'He Will REIGN!!! Every KNEE to HIM shall BOW!!'"

"I'd like to get off this subject without seeming to run away from it, so will say simply that Aunt Fran's effort comes across to me as basically arrogant, e.g., reflecting the attitude 'I'm right therefore. . .' – My father's position, as I see it, is entirely different and for my perceptions lacks even an element of arrogance, simple terror dominating his emotions so completely: 'I'm right because it would be so horrible if I were wrong.'"

"It seems to me that magic thinking, a term which, as I

use it, applies to the religious attitude as such, has an aspect which requires careful treatment before we go much further. There are various ways to describe it, so I'll just take the one that comes to me first. Since the magical/religious attitude is characterized by renunciation of objective inquiry in favor of the charismatic, it follows that the leadership of such movements will be limited to a small minority with a gift of facile formulation of phrases and terms. This preselection dictates the rest, meaning that with time the slicker ones gain the upper hand not by virtue of virtue, so to speak, but rather on the basis of lingual skills and shrewdness in dealing with potential or real threats to their domination. It's not for nothing that such organizations based on personal charisma split into 'divisions' when some newcomer, whether raised in the group or come to it from outside, challenges, in the name of the Holy Spirit, the existing distribution of power. All the splinter groups then claim exclusive possession to the TRUTH and the evil is in position to infect any who have been hitherto uninvolved or neutral. This splits families, often forever, and it's not possible, at least it wasn't in my case, to put a finger on the real culprit (named 'magic thinking' in my case) until one has passed through adolescence and probably early into technical adulthood."

"For me intellectual dishonesty is simply a subdivision of our old friend magic thinking: the obligation of the sectarian (and magic thinker) to *believe* everything presented to him by the leadership of whatever organization, sect, faction, party or movement he has let himself in for (or to!). Whereas the normal procedure when a stranger presents you with something allegedly superior to whatever it is you've done with up to then ... is to examine what is offered, and checking it out carefully as far as your own skills permit, e.g., hiring an expert (architect, plumber, geologist if you're buying a house)."

"With charisma-dependent choices you are *prohibited* from any rational examination or analysis. The guy who is selling his farmland cheap because of untreatable chemical pollution will likely come up with some modification of the 'without faith it is impossible to please Him' ploy. Simple people often take the reluctance of the unknown purveyor of unknown goods to let them be checked by an independent expert, as a kind of perverse sincerity, showing that he doesn't want to degrade his movement to an object of scrutiny from outsiders who lack respect for the high ideals on which it is allegedly based."

"Another approach is known as 'Pascal's Wager,' named after the French mathematician Blaise Pascal who 'flourished' in the late 16th century. His 'wager' went something like this: we cannot know if God exists; but if we believe in Him, He will take us to heaven when we die; whereas, if we don't believe in Him, He'll shoo us off to hell when we die. Therefore, the prudent man will believe to achieve the one and avoid the other."

"Somewhere I smell the armpits of Jehovah/Yahweh in this and leave you to supply your own interpretation. This mentality permeates the Bible, Job being the most striking example [Job 1: 6-22]. You will recall that in order to win a bet with Satan, made by Yahweh over morning coffee in heaven, that His servant Job would never curse Him whatever Satan might do to poor old Job, and that after Job had lost property, family and health without cursing Yahweh, the latter rewarded him with (I believe it was) double the number of pigs + goats + chickens + wives and children. However disgusting the value system here portrayed may be considered to seem, to me it is one of the most charming (!) portrayals of the ancient near-eastern value system."

"I rather hope that my deliberately chosen rambling style will still have betrayed my thoughts on magic thinking at least this far. It seems to me that if you want to program your computer for magic thinking, you would do well to regard it as indivisible, in the sense that as such it determines the nature and quality of the whole of the rest, very much like multiplying by zero in algebra. You cannot, like the little boy in H. C. Andersen's 'the Emperor's New Clothes,' say the king is naked because everybody else swears he's not and since the concept of nakedness is sufficiently subjective to make majority opinion decisive, your only option is to remain silent while the mob gorges itself on whatever spectacle is being presented to it at the moment."

"If the preceding paragraph seems to you to be (latently) anti-middle-of-the-roadism then I can assure you that this was entirely intentional." – "What Aunt Fran and my father have done, which led to my formulation, 'they are right, therefore they needn't be honest,' is to make packages of units of experience and, like a dog trained by the narcotics police to sniff out hidden caches of the substance they suspect is being smuggled, to condemn without deliberation or reflection anything which doesn't pass their white-on-white screening filter.

To continue the analogy of the sniffing dog, they accept its suspicion as proof of unacceptability and see no reason to forward the stuff to the central laboratory for definitive molecular analysis. Now you can do just that, but you cannot, by my lights report the sniffing dog's nose work as a chemical analysis. This latter trick is what I'm accusing Aunt Fran and Dad of doing."

"The dividing line to me is as follows: you are free to report analytical findings which are incomplete, but you are not free to report them as if they *were* complete. A stockbroker who gives his customers advice which he himself never follows will eventually defeat himself because of what I call 'dishonesty.' As Abe Lincoln so well put it, 'you can't fool all the people all the time.'"

"The difference between facts and their interpretation is illustrated by the history of 'Darwinism.' Darwin's contemporary opponents began by rejecting the notion in all of its forms as incompatible with 'the facts,' the latter being mostly such as were/are to be found at the beginning of Genesis. Today even fundamentalists need 'Wheaton professors' to supply hot air for the alleged stabilizing of their positions. Darwin's theory doesn't explain all the known facts, but any interpretation of them based on a priori rejection of Darwin's views is simply silly and wrong."

"The concept of a priori rejection, based on varying criteria known only to the acceptor or rejecter, is the basis of my charge against Aunt Fran and Dad. Neither of them has any willingness to submit his or her views to any third (or even second) party, much less to a discussion. And the amount of truth-stretching required by such a procedure should be self-descriptive, in fact is just that, as I see it."

"In principle, the 'Wheaton professor' and the Harold and Aunt Fran type are, respectively, more (and less) sophisticated products of the same disease: the manipulation of facts for private reasons not communicable to the unenlightened. The defect is complex, the diagnosis simple: in all of earth or heaven there is no force, instance, authority or source which can bring home a new fact or interpretation not in harmony with his preconceptions to a fanatical person."

18

MY CONVERSION

I finished grad school in May 1995, graduating with a social sciences Ph.D. in business administration. Moving across country from Arizona to Michigan kept me busy, but also allowed time to reflect on what was now several years of inter-continental written conversations with Bud. In retrospect, I was attempting to straddle two positions, to simultaneously ride two horses. Some of this dissonance was focused on the (dis)honesty of fanatical people and their unwillingness to consider whether they might be wrong.

I wrote to Bud...."Your formulation was that they (my father, grandfather and great aunt), and others of that ilk, are guilty of 'the manipulation of facts for private reasons not communicable to the unenlightened' and that 'there is no force, instance, authority or source which can bring home a new fact or interpretation not in harmony with his preconceptions to a fanatical person.' I have to admit I agree with your characterizations."

I continued ..."When my parents visited us a couple weeks ago I told them about a few of my misgivings regarding the Bible, e.g., the rapes, killings, etc., that the Israelites wrought in God's name; the apparent capriciousness of God in dealing with the various peoples of the earth; the murder of the planet's population with the exception of Noah and his crew; the rescue of Lot, who was willing to give his daughters up to the men of the village even though the visiting angels could have 'up and flown away;' the treatment of gays and homosexuals both in biblical times and today and the origin of their 'disorder' whether genetic or from eating the wrong foods (I'm joking of course) or, as one of the faculty members at Michigan State University believes, 'held in Satan's grip' (something which can be 'healed' when the afflicted one turns back to God), and so on. – My parents can't explain away or answer any of my doubts or questions. They do however unequivocally believe in their God and 'know' that one day all these things will be made clear to them. Their attitude is evidenced in words approximately like the following: 'God in his infinite wisdom has left these little conundrums unrevealed, but someday we'll know all.'"

I continued ... "I never considered, nor was I given a chance to think, that there might not be a god or God. Instead, I examined life from the perspective that God's existence was factual. This was a 'fact' that I never thought of examining until fairly recently. Thus, I don't know if my boyhood belief was based on emotion. – All I can think of right now is the gullibility of children, and how parents ought not to take advantage of it."

"My parents are very sincere and well-meaning. But by embracing the Bible as God's Word and acting as if this divine truth equals external reality and facts, they, or at least their position, can aptly be described as arrogant. So, to rephrase what I think you've been attempting to communicate, their position is dishonest – in the sense that they define their position to be The Truth, and discount whatever contradicts this truth based on the truth itself. They have no concern for what, from a researcher's [i.e., scientist's] viewpoint I call triangulation, i.e., that 'truth' is manifested only after a series of studies performed on different populations, using different data collection methods and different researchers, at different points in time, etc.; and that truth is only defined by what fails to be disproved. When I ask my parents a question about a point in the Bible, all they can do is point to other biblical passages and it's a vicious circle that makes me tired and sad."

"I do find it difficult to believe," I said, "that the universe, that life, exists without a catalyst. Regardless, if there is a creator, they certainly made their presence difficult to detect. – This situation leaves me uncomfortable. The rug of reality in one large dimension of my life has been jerked out from underneath my feet, and I've yet to recover my sense of balance. I often feel confused as to what principles should guide my life. At times I feel like an abandoned child and at the same time quite happy with my new-found perspective. While many former suspicions and doubts have been alleviated, new ones have risen in their place."

"ONE OF THE reasons I've been so slow in writing over the past several months is that I've experienced a number of fairly deep bouts of depression, although I'm not sure that I'd be diagnosed as such, clinically speaking. – I've just felt 'heavy-hearted.' Although I have emerged from it fairly recently, I believe the source of this depression is my lack of belief in 'something or someone.' I often feel like a ship without a rudder. My former belief in God was the cause of my belief in my own immortality and my belief that there was somebody or something more powerful than I was; these provided comfort. Today, I'm envious and incredulous when I meet people for whom the topic of the existence of god or God is not all that important. I'm almost of the opinion that my prior belief in a non-existent God is in some ways preferential to my current situation, sort of an 'ignorance is bliss' attitude."

I closed by saying: "I've recently picked up a copy of the amateur's monthly 'Sky & Telescope.' On the front cover and inside are mind-boggling pictures taken by the Hubble Space Telescope of the Eagle Nebula (M16). As I consider these pictures, I can't help but think of Richard Feynman's comment, from the copies you sent of a few pages of James Gleick's (1992, p. 372) book, *Genius*,[1] that 'this fantastically marvelous universe, this tremendous range of time and space and different kinds of animals, and all the different planets, and all these atoms with all their motions, and so on, all this complicated thing can merely be a stage so that God can watch human beings struggle for good and evil – which is the view that religion has. The stage is too big for the drama!' – And so my fight goes on."

19

BUD REPLIES AFTER I REACH ESCAPE VELOCITY

B ud replied soon after receiving my letter. "It gave and gives me profound satisfaction," he said, "to realize that after years of struggle (not that the subject matter isn't worth the time) you have decided that a course of intellectual evasion and rationalization of facts in the form of a religion-based Procrustean bed is not for you. Procrustes, as you may remember, in Greek mythology was the giant who forced each passing traveler to lie down on his (P's) bed; if too short for it, P. stretched him until he was long enough; if too long, P. chopped off the feet and as much of the legs as needed."

"I must admit I had my doubts from time to time as your naturally tender spirit weighed position and counterposition in the desperate hope of finding a middle ground which would spare the feelings (primarily of your parents, I had supposed) of those near and dear but unwilling, or unable, or both, to see how their position blocks the growth, even the possibility of growth, of the child's spirit and character. You commented on this point specifically in your own formulation."

"One point I *must* permit myself, and that is your report of the depressive feelings which accumulate as the result of your decision to face facts. In two lines you convinced me of the genuineness of your position, which you couldn't have done in 200 pages of script lacking this element. If my own experiences, and those of writers I've come to trust are any guide, I would expect that your depression, being based on facts rather than emotional projections, will remain, forcing you to return to the facts regularly, somewhat in the style of someone chewing on a piece of gristle. Why must God insist on playing devil's advocate? Why, with the hundreds of zillions of prayers addressed Him constantly does He answer none? And now to the mail box with these lines." – Bud

20

BUD'S RESPONSE TO MY
DEPRESSIVE FEELINGS

Three months later, Bud followed up: "You've been much on my mind, especially since you wrote about 'depression-like feelings' associated with your abandonment of the 'fruits and flowers,' not to say comforts, of magic thinking. In my vocabulary, magic thinking is the same thing, or seems to be, as what Jacques Monod calls 'animism' in his book *Chance and Necessity*.[1] If, as I am convinced, man made God in his own image, it stands to reason that he would continue along this path and go on to surround his creature ("God") with a religion, now one favoring constant enmity with neighbors (Yahweh), now the "God and Father of our Lord, Jesus Christ," as Paul [the Apostle] once formulated it."

"If I'm anywhere near right in this matter, your depressive feelings reflect the loss of an entity which came into being in the first place as part of a sincere effort on man's part to dream up a theological explanation for the miseries of life. For many people, the scientific explanation is inaccessible, and so they curse not only the *facts* which science digs up, but even more vehemently science's attempts to *explain* these facts. So if I am right, loss of religion is like the loss of a pacifier to an infant of six months who is addicted to it, or, to change the metaphor, like the loss of a scab over a superficial wound, the scab designed to prevent infection and loss of bodily fluid during the healing of the wound beneath."

"The pacifier and the scab share many characteristics, but their central function is to maintain as many functions and forms as possible during a phase of transition in and around a wound or (pacifier) impermanent condition. The emotional and logical accouterments of this process aren't analyzed because it is more convenient to ignore them and function as a legalist. And so, I suspect, your parents don't like to discuss these matters because instinct tells them they are doomed for all time to defend a closed system impervious to facts, or then even manipulate the facts to (as they pathetically hope) salvage their body of beliefs and prejudices."

21

COMING CLEAN TO MOM

Well, Bud was right about my parents. My mom, sister and her young child visited me in Michigan during my first year as a professor. As gently as I could, I told my mother of some of the changes in my beliefs, from what she and my father had taught me, to something I could live with: something that didn't offend my sense of logic or sense of rightness in terms of the pain and suffering that was experienced daily in the world. Something that didn't require mental acrobatics of which I was no longer capable. There is no other way to characterize my sharing of this news; it was devastating to her.

I had provided my parents clues, some not too subtle, as to my new set of beliefs, and pondered the ramifications of stating them outright, unsolicited. However, since they lived seven hours away by car, and we didn't see each other all that often, I'd been reluctant to tell them over the phone. However, when my mother was visiting, it became clear to me that I couldn't avoid 'coming clean.' For example, I wasn't going to pray before meals with her as I'd done all my life up to that point. I'm unsure of what the topic of discussion was ... I can however visualize the setting: when I said that I no longer believed in God, Mom asked: 'so, do you deny your salvation at age five?' For my mother, this was an important question, because she believed that once a person was saved, they couldn't reverse it, i.e., they were always saved. I responded, 'No. I was a naive and gullible little boy and earnest in my beliefs. But I probably would have believed in anything or anybody who was presented so earnestly and systematically by my parents and their friends.'

The discussion on this subject didn't last long, because my sister declared that we shouldn't talk about it in front of her kid, which was ironic since they were age five or six. I countered that children ought to be presented with the fact that there are many alternative beliefs, and that they'd have to make up their own minds, given that nobody could demonstrate absolute truth. That suggestion didn't go over well, but I felt like an immense psychological weight had fallen off my shoulders, like I'd been emancipated. And the feeling wasn't short lived.

The next morning, I noticed with some feeling of guilt, that my mother had a pile of used tissues by the side of her bed. Her eyes were red; she'd been crying. The cause was the rather intense exchange the previous evening on what I believed, what I didn't believe, and why. In essence, I had denied the existence of the God she claimed to know and love. And that, despite her and my father's best efforts over my lifetime to inculcate in me that same knowledge and love of the God of the Bible.

So, on one hand, I felt a sense of relief because there was no advantage to, or real possibility of, hiding my changed beliefs. This, because the daily religious exhortations which were so much a natural part of our daily conversations, and prayers at the dinner table, were now troublesome for me. However, her emotional pain hurt me. It's not that I had any internal need to behave in an extravagantly rebellious manner, but simply that after years of contemplation, I had reached a conclusion that was based on reality as best I could ascertain it.

BUD'S THOUGHTS ON
TELLING MOM

A month or so after my mother, sister and her child returned home, I sent Bud a note describing my conversations with my mother, and the relief I felt in doing so. Soon afterward, he responded: "What impresses me so favorably is the fact that you pursued the truth relentlessly but without haste and without flinching when your reflections brought you to a position you probably hadn't foreseen coming to. I remember being genuinely astonished at the contents of your earlier letters, which showed a relentlessness of aim and a clarity of purpose which even someone averse to insight must admire. Probably the reason you achieved your first goal after less than two years, at least that's how it comes across to me. But you have seen the damage wreaked, especially on character, by the cultivation of magic thinking and, in my judgment, done the only possible thing."

VISITING BUD AND
CONFRONTATION WITH MY FATHER

During summer 1996, I visited Bud at his home in Basel, Switzerland. This was the first time I had seen him face-to-face since I was a small child. This visit was the first of several trips I made to Basel during the next three years. To be able to talk with a family member openly about what I believed and why, and about the world and universe, without fear of reproof or dismissal was refreshing and uplifting. At the same time, I was saddened to see the effects Parkinson's was having on my friend and uncle. How grateful I am for those visits, the continuance of our written correspondence and our mutual striving for understanding.

However, the joy, relief and enlightened feelings I experienced in Basel were somewhat lessened when I returned to Michigan and drove east for my youngest sister's upcoming wedding in New York. The night before her wedding, my father and I had a semi-furious conversation in the basement of my parents' house.

As I characterized it in a letter to Bud, "Our conversation was of belief in a God or gods. Dad may have started the dialog (perhaps a misnomer, as you'll see shortly!) by saying something approximately like the following: 'What I don't understand is why you guys are still bothered by the subject of God and the Christian faith. If you don't believe in it why are you consumed by it and still so angry about it?' (My perception is that because Dad 'knows' that his God exists, he interprets our 'inability to dismiss the topic with finality' as evidence that there is truth to his beliefs.) I said that the topic itself did not have any peculiar hold on us, but what makes us angry, even now, is the forced feeding of doctrine which began while we were in the womb and which continued systematically and dogmatically once we emerged from it. In addition, we aren't angry with God because there isn't any 'God' to be angry with, but we are angry with the messenger and the messenger's method of adamant indoctrination. I stated that he had no right to force his beliefs down his children's throats when he couldn't demonstrate the validity of his beliefs. He disagreed. At that point, (we were both over-tired), I got a bit pissed off, because I was thinking of my sister's child, who has been living under my parents' roof with her for two or three years. My response to his disagreement was to use a fictional example to make my point."

"I said: 'So if tomorrow (my sister) converts to some Eastern religion (unfamiliar to us), which demands the daily ritual of kneeling and praying to some god (other than Jesus and His Father) ... you won't have a problem with her belief as long as she believes it fervently and 'knows she's found the truth' – and thus it's okay if she inculcates (her five year old child) with her new-found belief.' He said he probably would have a problem with it, but couldn't provide a satis-factory reason why. Things deteriorated a bit after that, I was pretty angry, and when I quoted a Bible verse to him he said 'don't you quote from the Bible, when you hate both the book and its author.'"

"The next morning I clarified a few points with him. First, I said I had every right to quote from the Bible, as it is a book and thus quotable, and that although my perspective of its authorship differed from his, that wouldn't prevent me from including it in my arsenal and quoting from it whenever I saw fit. He conceded I was right. I also said I didn't hate his God – I just believed that 'He' was a fictional character and thus my feelings toward 'Him' were one of indifference. My last point was a reiteration of the idea that my anger today is fed by memories of him force-feeding his religion to his children, and that (my sister's child) was receiving the same treatment today and had no say in the matter."

I continued, "We also talked of your (Bud's) recent letter to him. And we looked at the [letter] my father wrote where he ... claimed 'the Christian's responsibility being greater [than the non-Christian] due to the greater knowledge that he claims.'"

My father also said "he was going to respond [to Bud's letter], in part, by using the following illustration to explain God's apparent inaction to human suffering on earth. 'If a person creates a little figure out of wood, say a dog or boy or elephant, and decides that he doesn't like his creation, he (as creator) can do whatever he wills with that creation, including destroy it. And the created figure would have no say in the matter.' My response was that his analogy was okay as far as it went but was inadequate. I said to make it a valid analogy, the person would have to create many figures, give them life and free will, and that the creator would have to label himself as omnipotent, omniscient and just. Furthermore the creator would have to describe himself as being the very essence of love. And the creator would then have to prejudicially segregate his creatures into groups that he favored and disfavored, and murder some of those that were in his disfavor, and so on."

"Well, I don't believe he'll try that analogy (again), but who knows. We left the topic of 'parental right to inculcate' alone, I think, perhaps, both of us realized that to pursue it further might leave our relationship in tatters.'"

24

MY RELIEF IS ALMOST PALPABLE

I composed a quick note to Bud after visiting him in Basel during summer 1996: "I looked briefly back at some of the letters we've exchanged," I wrote, "and am amazed to see how my perspective re: God/god has changed over the past few years. I'm also amazed as I think back to our discussions on your balcony in Basel, to see how true the perspective of the world and its inhabitants seems without the confounding factor of a G/god. All the facts and knowledge known to me fit together so much better without the existence of the vengeful Yahweh and without magic thinking! I'm also more content today to, as our cousin so aptly put it, 'settle for constant revision of working hypotheses on the basis of available information.' And being able to admit uncertainty about the origins of the universe and life on this planet, is, in some strange way, empowering, in comparison to defiant, in-your-face statements of contradictory 'facts' from the Bible. As I noted in my previous letter to you, I felt an immense relief after unequivocally stating my beliefs to my mother, and the relief continues. I've finally declared my intellectual independence from my parents and their bridling beliefs, and the relief is almost palpable."

25

MY PARENTS' REACTIONS AND MY
RESPONSE

My parents never did accept my claims of
changed belief. In one letter, my mother wrote
"I don't like this so-called 'polite' relationship.
You speak against the One I love above all others, the One
who cared enough for me to rescue me from Satan's hell and
whose love and faithfulness I have enjoyed daily even
though I've failed him daily." She continued, "You have no
idea how much it hurt my heart not to be able to thank the
Lord at your table (though I did in my heart). He truly is
despised and rejected of men. I'm just sorry it has to be that
way in our family."

She continued, "You mention about a monster God; I
hate that expression, it cuts deep into my heart and though
you mention the flood, don't forget Noah preached 120 years
and no one would believe him. Then, when he did go into
the ark the Lord left the door open another seven days.
There is nothing, nothing, nothing harder than man's heart.
– We continue to pray for you; thankfully you can't put a
stop to that."

She further argued, "Your Dad wasn't an alcoholic or a

child molester or unfaithful to me or you, was he? Well, maybe it would do you good to talk to some people who were brought up that way; seems to me your problems were insignificant compared to theirs." – I didn't respond to her at that time, but all I could think was that adamantly forcing one's beliefs on children was a form of child abuse, which was unwise given that the child would eventually figure it out if they were at all inquisitive.

So, parental denials of me discarding my religious faith continued, as did my efforts to get them to understand why I could no longer believe as they did and to achieve some level of equilibrium in our relationship. For example, my mother wrote me in 2001 to say, "You know as well as I that to be absent from the body is to be present with the Lord. So that's where ... grandpa and grandma on both sides, are – so for you to say differently was unkind." I responded: "You've said a lot in that sentence, and I can't allow you to make such an adamant statement without providing a rebuttal. First, you apparently haven't listened to my statements about my beliefs, and you apparently haven't read the contents of (or if read, have disregarded) my letters to Dad and you a couple of years ago. Second, I don't 'know' any of what you claim in your statement. Further, I would like to gently remind you that you also don't *know* anything about what you claimed in your statement."

My father, also, continued to ignore my claims of discarded religious belief. So, in a letter to my father, dated October 2002, I said: "I'm going to respond as clearly as I know how, first, by pointing to the warts and scabs in your belief system, and second, by charging you with being intellectually dishonest. And, to use a boxing metaphor, I won't be pulling any punches. I'll keep the curses to myself, but my purpose in this note is to pull out the magnifying glass and examine your god in all its lurid detail."

"One of the primary themes of my comments to you over the past several years has been in the general area of the god you worship. You say I exhibit hatred toward Him. But, I don't believe the god of the Bible exists. Instead, I exhibit hatred toward the ideas espoused by people who worship this imaginary god, because this belief is poisonous to the mind, especially young, gullible minds."

"You, as a fundamentalist Christian take the Bible verbatim – do you not? Here's why I am repulsed by your belief system. I'll refer to both the King James and J.N. Darby versions [of the Bible].

Murder: Genesis 7:4: last part of the verse: 'and every living substance that I have made will I destroy from off the face of the earth' (KJV). J.N.D.'s version: 'For in yet seven days I will cause it to rain on the earth forty days and forty nights; and every living being which I have made will I destroy from the ground.'

Murder: Genesis 38: ~6-10: 'And Er . . . was wicked in the sight of Jehovah, and Jehovah slew him.' Later, in verse 10, Onan is killed by Jehovah for cumming on the ground, i.e., spilling his seed. (KJV).

Murder: Exodus 12:29: 'the Lord smote all the firstborn in the land of Egypt' (KJV). J.N.D.'s version: 'And it came to pass at midnight Jehovah smote all the firstborn in the land of Egypt.' Later, in Chapter 14, verse 4, the Lord tells Moses that he will 'harden Pharaoh's heart, that he may pursue after them; and I will glorify myself in Pharaoh . . .'

– I can only assume that the 'glorify myself' part means that he'll kill many more Egyptian soldiers in the sea.

Murder: As you probably know, Deuteronomy is full of orders to commit murder. A couple of examples: Deuteronomy 22:22: (KJV; J.N.D.) 'Kill adulterers,' Deuteronomy 13:1-5. I'll paraphrase here: ~ 'kill a prophet' if he is a 'dreamer of dreams.'

Hemorrhoids: Oh, yeah! 1 Samuel 5:9: 'and He [Jehovah] smote the men of the city, both small and great, and hemorrhoids broke out upon them' (J.N.D.). Wow, that's a nice touch!

Murder of children: 'And he (Elisha) turned back, and looked on them (the children), and cursed them in the name of Jehovah. And there came forth two she-bears out of the wood, and tore forty two children' (2 Kings 2:24, J.N.D.)."

I continued, "There are literally hundreds of additional examples of murder, torture, disease, people being burned; these all perpetrated by the god you worship – but I'll stop for now. So, if you've decided to read this far, I suspect that you'll be saying something like: ~ 'But now we're in a new dispensation, a new era ... just look at the New Testament and Jesus.' – OK, let's have a look."

Jesus as a progenitor of violence: 'Think not that I am come to send peace on earth: I came not to send peace, but a sword' (Matthew 10:34, KJV).

Jesus promises violence: 'The Son of man shall send his angels, and they shall gather out of his kingdom all offences, and those that practice lawlessness; and they shall cast them into the furnace of fire; and there shall be the weeping and the gnashing of teeth' (Matthew 13:41-42, J.N.D.).

Jesus gives permission for cruelty to animals: 'and Jesus [immediately] allowed them. And the unclean spirits going out entered into the swine, and the herd rushed down the steep slope, into the sea (about two thousand), and were choked in the sea' (Mark 5:12-13, J.N.D.).

Jesus says you should fear God because he may send you to hell: Luke 12:5

Jesus promises hell-fire: Jesus says 'unless any one abide in me he is cast out as the branch, and is dried up; and they gather them and cast them into the fire, and they are burned' (John 15:6, J.N.D.).

"Well," I wrote, "I'll stop there. You seem to focus on the fruits and flowers of your belief system; I'll focus on the blood and guts; somebody has to. The passages above beg a simple question: 'Why do you accept behavior of your god that you wouldn't accept from your neighbor?'"

"You have asked ... 'where is your joy?' I ask you ... 'why do you ignore the violent, murderous, capricious, and juvenile side(s) of the god you worship?' In your latest letter, you say 'I enjoy sharing my faith.' How do you share your faith? By telling people that they will go to hell forever if they don't believe in your god? If not, why? You say I lack joy. I'll admit to a reasonable dose of pessimistic realism, not to cynicism, but in my opinion it's better than believing in a murderous god."

I continued, "I think I'm correct in stating that every day you probably enjoy the idea that Jesus will return to earth and take you to heaven. Do you, for even an instant, think about all the people who will be left behind and the fate to which your belief system has in store for them? It's preposterous! You get to go to heaven and walk streets of gold; everybody else gets tortured in hell forever." – I didn't receive a response to these questions.

IN MY RESPONSE to another of my mother's letters, I also said: "What do I believe? I'm glad to tell you! I don't know if the god you believe in exists. I have no reason to believe he does. It doesn't matter if I'd like him to exist or not. My wanting, one way or the other, changes nothing. I'm not an atheist; an atheist believes there is no G/god. I believe we don't have any evidence of a G/god, nor do we have any evidence there is a hereafter. I certainly cannot believe in the God of the Bible; he is too violent for me. The Bible describes him as a creator of hell. As I've said to people who ask; my mind is no longer capable of going through the mental acrobatics required to believe in the God of the Bible."

As children, we sang the following song – I don't know the source:

"The B-I-B-L-E,
Oh that's the book for me;
I stand alone on the Word of God,
The B-I-B-L-E!"

Today, some conservative Christians and others, like-minded, are attempting to ban books from libraries, schools and other venues in the USA. The reasons cited for exclusion include gratuitous violence, grooming, sex, two papas, two mommas and who knows what else! So, why not ban the book on which I largely learned to read, the Bible? From beginning to end, it's filled with descriptions of a cruel, vengeful, violent god, either perpetrating violence himself, or commanding his followers to do so. Many people attempt to differentiate between the god of the Old Testament and Jesus, but a close examination shows, that Jesus' character isn't very commendable, especially his attitude toward those who didn't worship him. Biblical violence is stunning in its scope and depth; it's depressing. Slavery is condoned, women are subjugated and treated as chattel, animals mistreated, and God's appetite for murder and mayhem is seemingly insatiable.

At this point in my life, my primary concern is not for the contents of the Bible itself. After all, there are also charming stories in the Bible and even lessons to be learned. But, for people, yes, like my father, who accept the Bible as the unerring word of the god he worships, what is the effect of this belief? If a person accepts the biblical culture of violence, does it affect their personality and character? If violence is normalized in the Bible, and in the songs sung as an accompaniment, is there not a significant chance of spillover of that violence into the speech, attitudes and even the actions of its believers? To me, the answer is yes, because I've lived it.

26

AGNOSTIC-DENIER VERSUS AGNOSTICS

During summer 1996, my parents made a trip to Washington state to visit relatives, during which my father visited with one of his first cousins, who lived in northern Europe. Upon his return, my father wrote a letter to his brother, Bud, which expressed some fear: "He (their cousin) threw one curve at me when he said that (my wording) 'instead of God making man in His image, man has made God in his image.' I wasn't able to perceive the message at the time, but since have realized its meaning. And it scares me."

My own response to my father's expressed fear was incredulousness, because Bud had communicated many times over many years these same sentiments, essentially that the reason the Christian's god is so violent is that man created him, and since human history is so full of violence and war, the god whom they invented is also violent. My father's comment led to an exchange of letters between my father, on one side, and Bud and their cousin on the other. I was cc'd on these various letters but felt it wise to stay on the sidelines as a silent observer. What follows are a few highlights and excerpts – a short version of this exchange.

From Bud and his cousin: "We share an avid distaste for claims of Absolute Truth, particularly when such claims are accompanied by a willing disregard for knowledge."

My father responded by saying, "It's clear that our beliefs are irreconcilable since you guys reject the Book I accept as truth." Then, for reasons I cannot fully fathom, except for lack of self-awareness and undiluted arrogance, he included a "poem" he had written that had fourteen stanzas. I'll only include three. The title of the poem was "Absolutely!"

> 1st: "God has a book of absolutes,
> And every word is true;
> It's called the Holy Bible,
> It's God's own words to you."

> 9th: "Another precious absolute
> Found in the Holy Word;
> That God is man's creator;
> Evolution is absurd."

> 12th: "But O, another absolute
> Tells of a place called hell
> Where those who spurn the Savior's grace
> Eternally shall dwell."

He might as well have poked his brother and cousin in their eyes with sticks: "In your 'poem,'" his cousin wrote, "you dismiss with a flick of the wrist as it were, evolution, calling it 'absurd.' Have you ever bothered to find out the first thing about it? Your dismissal is, I suggest, the product of total ignorance – in the full implication of ignoring the overwhelming accumulation of facts. You know better, you're fully qualified to bestow your expert opinion, having studied all the available biological evidence, is that it? It seems to me that you don't have to know because you believe instead, and that is so bloody arrogant of you!"

Bud took a different tack: "What I mean to say can in prospect be covered as one theme: how do I distinguish truth from falsehood?" He characterized fundamentalists like my father as holding "the absolute conviction that their interpretation of reality is correct simply because it's theirs, and let facts be damned." Further that "the religious person ... simply rejects any new finding which contravenes his codes and belies and curses the scientists who interrupt his metaphysical slumbers." And finally, "there is something about religion which makes its adherents think of themselves as qualified per se to make meaningful judgments of the moral and ethical aspects of other people's lives."

My father's response: "I know it's offensive, but you know that without question, I believe the Bible. Yes, you can call my belief ignorance. I understand. I know of no acceptable way of addressing this matter with you without irritating you more."

In Bud's response, he said: "I can see how religion serves a vital need in you and others of your persuasion, and I would not even attempt to restrict your continued cultivation of it, were it not for the fact that you feel obligated not only to promulgate it among other people, but also to criticize them for the varying degrees of deviation from your line, which should be your private option and not something to beat other people with." – "Whether something you advocate is true or not seems to be a matter of indifference to you, or at best merely a source of recurring irritation. But you will have to live with the knowledge that the vast majority of people would not find themselves able to accept your promulgation of a very private doctrine as a source of all Truth. I myself think that the truth is one thing and recognition of it is quite another. You are continually getting yourself into logical traps because you have committed yourself to 'believing' an unchanging and unchangeable body of doctrine."

He continued, "The decision to believe something which has not been proved or even cannot be proved, is not something which can be treated lightly. It is, in fact, an ethical question of the highest rank, since unquestioning acceptance of a pre-formed creed prevents you, among other things, from revising your doctrines and beliefs to fit new insights and even to tolerate new insights." – "Fundamentalists seem to think they must see to it that life isn't made too easy for their children, but I assure them that fate creates enough trouble and difficulty for everyone that there has never been a case in all history of a deficit of these commodities anywhere."

My father's response, referring to Bud's two paragraphs just cited: "The rest of your letter is just so controversial that I'll withhold comment." And, "it seems amazing to me that, in context, I shouldn't share my thoughts and beliefs with others, yet you're licensed to ridicule me and mine."

THIS EXCHANGE REMINDS me of a brilliant cartoon from 1997 by the cartoonist David Wiley Miller in his cartoon "Non Sequitur." In it, two men face each other, both holding large sandwich boards. The man on the right holds a sandwich board that says "The truth as I see it." The other man's board says: "The facts as they are." The title of the cartoon: "The Irresistible Force Meets the Immovable Object."

27

BUD'S ASSESSMENT

I had visited Bud in Basel during summer 1996, argued with my father about his adamant religiosity later that summer, and been a by-stander in the discussion between my father and his brother and cousin. While I had remained on the sidelines of the philosophical arguments described in the previous chapter, I did hear from Bud regarding this resurgence of the nearly sixty year religious war between him and his brother, for which I was at least partly responsible.

He wrote: "I don't have anything new to report on the theological battlefield, and suppose that the 'sides' are resting and repleting the oxygen supplies of heart and soul. I'm convinced that Charles hasn't grasped the enormity of the complaints we have submitted for his consideration and is still determined to maintain his claims for absolute inerrancy as to source and at least conditional inerrancy as to interpretation. Thus the old cycle of exaggeration of material submitted as dogma and forced upon children and stragglers who are either too innocent or too cowed and beaten to run away in search of a more salubrious environment. I search my memory of my own years as a believer and remember that even as a teenager I was convinced that any belief or set of beliefs worth its salt would establish and maintain itself without the dependence on intimidation."

"It is evident that we are dealing, so far as I can see, with the same problem, each from his particular coign of vantage: how to keep Charles off our backs theologically and philosophically while loving him as a person. I imagine he is hurting sufficiently to be unable to distinguish between self-description and proselytizing, at least for the time being."

"I find one feature which disturbs me (even if not terribly deeply) and that is his age. I was forty seven when I reached what has turned out to be at least so far, an adequate view of life and the cosmos. The sudden falling into place of all kinds of bits and particles of insight occurred within a few months – indeed I suspect weeks would be technically more exact. I replaced a crassly outdated 'Weltanschauung' with another which not only fits the facts as I know them but also satisfies me emotionally. It was delightful to see for the first time that God and gods have such evil characters because their characters come from the dung heap, and from odd cuttings from the operating room and the slaughterhouse and zoo."

"Confronted with a person dear to us who somewhere got and kept the notion that willful destruction of other human beings can be accepted as a character feature of a respectable God, you have to worry what might happen if he sees your point and then has to spend the rest of his days running away from reality, moving his bed away from the drooping ceiling instead of fixing the roof."

Later in the letter he wrote: "The basic bitch from my side also comes across clearly in your report: forcing religion upon one's own and other people's children. My objections to this aspect of the situation led to his [Charles] wondering why I complained about being indoctrinated in this way, since I've had plenty of time to clean up my emotional house since leaving the Meeting in my early twenties. He has, and I've told him so, a lot of explaining to do there. I never met anybody, no matter how otherwise beknighted or enlightened, who denied the concept of permanent damage to an organism by events in babyhood or childhood, and neuroendocrinology teaches us that damage to certain brain parts and functions is unavoidable when the mother is treated before parturition with substances which are either intrinsically harmful or become so at certain phases of development."

28

A PLEA FROM THE PAST

L ooking back at my partially accumulated bundle of correspondence between Bud and my father, and Bud and their father, I am amazed at how prescient he was in assessing my father's and grandfather's beliefs which are reflected in my own experiences with them.

Way back in May 1966, Bud, in a letter to my father, described their father, Harold, as "a wax dummy with a pre-recorded Bible in place of a soul."

"Dear Charles," he wrote, "It is frightening to me to imagine that as you grow older you might turn into someone like Dad; [a person who seems] to have retreated from reality between the pages of their Bibles, and from whom one gets only such reactions as can be readily fore-seen on the basis of their known prejudices and fixed points of judgment.

Judging from your last letter I would incline to think you are in danger of suffering, even you with your warmth and openness, the calcification and scarring of the soul which from my point of view is characteristic of those who have dedicated their lives to this religion. You can't talk with them about any real problem, because you know in advance that discussion is out of the question; you know their reactions and answers in advance; you are aware that their minds move like trains – only on tracks already fixed in place. Any reality, however obvious and naked it may be, which doesn't fit the tracks cannot by definition be recognized by them, any more than a train passing a lovely forest can turn off its course for a closer view.

Even the substitution of a tape-recorded Bible for a soul would be less tragic if they didn't carefully edit out all the parts which don't fit their tracks. – "Judge not, that ye be not judged" [Matthew 7:1] and about 80-90% of the rest of the Bible is scrupulously eliminated from their tapes – more accurately, never recorded in the first place. The reality of life, its tragedy, its complexity, its meaning, cannot even be confronted by these people. They are content, and I have no wish to disturb their contentment. I only ask them to leave me alone."

Bud ended his letter with a plea: "Brother – only brother – of mine, believe what you wish, follow your beliefs as you think well, but stay human, I beg you."

29

FAMILY DISCORD

The layers of family history continued to accumulate over decades. In one sense the flavor of our relationships remained unchanged. My parents continued to refuse my agnosticism, although they weren't very verbal about it. They acknowledged it but didn't accept it. As I stated in a letter to my mother: "I no longer believe as you do. I've tried to explain this to you and Dad, but it appears to me that you're not interested in what I believe, and in fact, choose to believe quite the reverse – that somehow the beliefs that you tried to inculcate in me as a child still hold."

They continued to pray for me; I continued to think of them. Most of our conversations, refutations, arguments, all part and parcel of a polite relationship lacking substance, continued unchanged and require little comment.

However, in one notable episode and its aftermath, the family gathered to celebrate my parents' fiftieth wedding anniversary in 2002, renting a house on Lake Huron near Bayfield, Ontario. The weekend was mostly peaceful until Sunday morning, when my parents gathered their grandchildren together and began to sing Sunday School songs and read the Bible to them. This occurred right in my presence and I interrupted the proceeding and caused a commotion. I was offended. I was angry. I was unkind.

I had previously explicitly told my parents that I would not stand idly by if I witnessed them proselytizing such as they were doing right then in front of me. In a letter to my father I had written: despite my protestations, "you continue to promulgate your 'truth' to unsuspecting and gullible children, and withhold your love from your kids when they're not behaving according to your private code of conduct. – Unless you would like a counter-point presented by me whenever I'm around to witness your propaganda campaign, you should keep your beliefs to yourself."

But it was an unhappy scene that day and I'm not overly proud of my actions. Silence followed. About three months later, my father sent me an email wherein he wondered "if we're going to hear from you?" He continued "we think we've accepted you as you are, in spite of your beliefs. You obviously feel we should keep our beliefs to ourselves." And, he pleaded, "is there any reason why we can't accept each other – in spite of differing beliefs? I know you won't accept our preaching, but I didn't think we were guilty of that."

My response wasn't all that gracious. "Perhaps I'll reply with more thoughts at a later date," I wrote, "but for now here's something to chew on."

"I don't like the deterioration in our relationship any more than you apparently do," I said. "I love you both but have intense feelings about seeing yet another generation experiencing the same demagoguery I did as a kid."

"When [one of my siblings] had an affair with their boss a few years ago, they came to me, devastated that they had received a letter from Mom containing the message: 'If you are going to continue to live in sin, perhaps you would be better off dead.'" – Wow, I thought to myself when I first heard this report, and here all along I thought my father was the extremist! How could a mother, whose DNA is essentially encoded to protect and love her children, think let alone utter such a thought?

"It's this sort of shit," I wrote, "that I remember when I see the seemingly innocent relationship where grandparents sit down with their grandchildren and sing about Jesus. The relationship-building activity (singing about Jesus) is NOT innocent. Instead, you build an emotional bond with undeveloped minds who don't have the capacity, the will or the knowledge to objectively evaluate the information that is being conveyed in the form of loving songs. You then put yourself in the position to wreak havoc in their lives later on if they do something of which you disapprove."

"Would you give me equal time with those children to tell them about the God of the old testament who allowed a she-bear to kill forty or more children? Or perhaps you could tell [your oldest grandson] that since he was the first-born, the angel would have murdered him when [the angel] went through during the scourges of Egypt."

I closed by saying: "You and Mom can believe what you want. But I can't stand idly by while you show innocent, gullible children only one side of the god you worship, especially given the potential for emotional blackmail that can conceivably take place at a later date and knowing first-hand the hurt that results." And I signed my name.

30

POLES APART: THE SAGA CONTINUES

My interactions with Bud, which primarily consisted of several face-to-face visits at his apartment in Basel, also included a visit by him to the USA. During fall 1997, he was ailing; Parkinson's was taking its toll. But he made the trip from Basel, Switzerland accompanied by his cousin, who lived in northern Europe, to Okemos, Michigan, where I was living at the time. He had a desire to visit places where he had grown up, in and around Detroit, and in nearby Ann Arbor where he had earned his undergraduate degree at the University of Michigan and achieved some level of intellectual independence from his parents. He also agreed to see my father and mother, who were excited to make the seven hour drive.

Bud arrived at my house accompanied by his cousin, who left him in my care for several days and returned several days later on his way back to Europe. Having Bud in my home was a wonderful, happy experience. At the same time, I could see the effects of Parkinson's in his ungainly gait and the constant trembling of his hands. He also suffered from episodes of stumbling and short-term bursts of an inability to keep his balance. But he was happy and his sense of humor and intellect were intact.

The incident I recall most vividly from those several days, was when my father and mother first arrived at the house. There we were, Bud and I, standing inside the front door, and in walked my father followed closely by my mother. This was the first time these brothers had seen each other in thirty five years!

After an exchange of smiles, greetings and hugs, and still standing just inside the front door of my home, my father, for reasons that still confound me, said:

"Bud, I have a bone to pick with you."

"What's that?" Bud asked.

"I have it from a reliable source that you were in the USA in the mid-1970s, and passed within ten miles of our house, and didn't call or stop by for a visit," said my father.

"I was upset with you for the way you were treating your boys!" came Bud's immediate and booming response.

My father, hearing Bud's retort, started to laugh, perhaps realized that he had for inexplicable reasons just dug up a religious familial shit-show from the past, and turned bright red. I shook my head and said nothing. But this interaction was perhaps a reminder to all who were present, that despite the familial warmth the two parties were still diametrically opposed in how they viewed life, the world and the cosmos.

THE REST of Bud's stay included a visit to the University of Michigan where he shared remembrances of his young adult days. Afterwards, we stopped in to a pub for a pint of beer, an experience I've never shared with my father. We also visited a nearby book store where he purchased several books. I look back fondly on this time with Bud. I was able to sit in on a few conversational exchanges between him and my father and mother. These exchanges reinforced how far apart they were in their world-views.

The last time I saw Bud was during the summer of 1998, when I visited him, once more in Basel. He died in the spring of 1999. His last couple of months were painful to watch from a distance. In July, the Swiss authorities allowed us into his apartment to sort through his belongings. I cried when I first saw the blood stains on the carpet where he had fallen, but it was comforting to be in his apartment where I best remembered him. In his death, I lost my best friend, a mentor and a relative who loved and cared enough for me to intercede and plead, on behalf of me and my brother, with my father all those years before, and who took the time and effort to hand write scores of letters to help me clearly understand the effects of the fanatical environment in which I had been raised.

Now, here in 2025, my father lives on, perhaps genetically programmed to live to one hundred. Our relationship has waxed and waned. We talk on the phone a couple of times a month, mostly about the weather and family. These calls last a couple of minutes with little substance. His dogmatic religious stance is as strong as ever and perhaps more belligerent. He often ends his phone calls with "the Lord be with you," even though I've asked him to refrain from these wishful proclamations. His latest Christmas card included the hand printed verse: "believe on the Lord Jesus and you will be saved," Acts 16:31.

All of his children and most of his grandchildren have been recipients of written or verbal condemnations of our life-decisions based on his private interpretation of the Bible. Most recently he expressed his disappointment to my brother, a man in his early sixties, for the length of his hair. But this example of his disapproval is a Miller-Lite of condemnations compared to his other proclamations. He has condemned us "for living in sin," unmarried, for our divorces, for how we think and behave, and for how we dress. He once called one of his now ex-daughter-in-laws, "Jezebel," and condemned her for "living in sin" with one of his sons. Other family members have been treated to months or years of silence to express his disapproval of the way they choose to live their lives. He's always right; never in doubt, with a level of arrogance that defines the high end of the arrogance scale.

Over the past several decades, he has taken to writing what he calls poems. Here is an example from 2001, after the September 11th attacks:

> "What happened today is NOTHING
> Compared to what's coming, my friend
> Those World Trade Towers, they tumbled
> The terror never seemed to end"

There are several more stanzas. Here's one from the middle, where he refers to the victims:

> "For eternity now they've entered,
> Such a sober reality;
> Solemn choice previously made:
> Heaven's bliss or hell's destiny!"

And here's the last stanza:

> "God's awful judgment is coming
> And none shall escape in that day!

Behold now's the accepted time,
Jesus is the truth and the way."

So, the god my father worships is jealous, judgmental, violent and murderous. He appears to be saying, 'if you think the attacks of September 11th, 2001 were bad, wait until my God gets ahold of you.' This is his brand of religious fanaticism. His character, to me, is deformed by his fanatical, fundamentalist beliefs. He claims absolute truth and those who don't believe in Him will be fucked for eternity by his god if they don't believe in Him. He believes he gets 'heaven's bliss' and everybody else, if they don't believe, will get hell, apparently because they deserve it. For me, he aptly fits the label of moral sadist.

My impressions? He is intellectually dishonest with himself, his children, grandchildren and others around him. His character is emotionally deformed by his fanatical beliefs. Clearly he can be a warm and friendly person, but the algebraic sum of his pluses and minuses, his warmth and his judgmental character which is formed by his fanatical beliefs, yield a negative result. Of the feelings I have for him, pity predominates.

31

PAIN AND SUFFERING OF MY MOM AND MY FRIEND

As dictated by our patriarchal religion, my mother did not play *the* preeminent role in our family home and history; that position was held by my father. But she played a very significant role, even if categorized technically by her religion as secondary. She was kind, mostly soft-spoken, discouraged about our familial infighting and violence, and missed her native Canadian home. Clearly she had episodes of denial. For example, she denied my denial of the fundamentalist Christian beliefs in which she and my father had done their best to inculcate me as a child.

My most enduring memories of her, perhaps because of their repeated occurrences, are of her sitting at the morning breakfast table reading her Bible after everybody had left, her head covered with a napkin. My most vivid memory is of her playing kickball with us in our backyard and laughing with glee as she rounded the bases in her flowing dress after she'd kicked the ball. She was considerate, kind and patient while also leaning toward being judgmental if you were able to probe her thoughts. She loved her Lord,

Jesus Christ, and I think her religion enabled her to be happy in spite of our familial strife.

Marilyn Krause, my mother, died of pancreatic cancer in 2004, after approximately eighteen months of significant pain and suffering. She decided not to take cancer treatments, having seen her younger sister die in her early sixties while suffering through a treatment regimen that made her sick, frail and her hair fall out. The last time I hugged Mom, she felt thin, weak, breakable. I could see her body betraying her will to live. She couldn't eat much beyond bland. The last time I talked with her on the phone, just a few days before she died, she talked about how much she loved to drink water. She said, "I just throw it up, but I love it so much I drink it anyway." – The last few days of her life were mentally hazy due to the morphine she received to stave off her pain.

I had nothing to do with the funeral arrangements and despise open coffin funerals, but there she was, on display; the only time I'd ever seen her wearing eye-liner and make-up. The funeral director spontaneously reminded me of a devious used car salesman with his pencil-thin mustache. I had a brief fantasy of punching him in his face. Was he the make-up artist?

I had a reserved seat in the front row for the service, and as I requested, it was on the side of the room next to an exterior door. When the first person, who I didn't recognize, started a solemn sermon about my mother in language that was steeped in religious wistfulness, I quietly rose and exited into the outdoors.

The funeral was in New York state. As I left the building, some late arrivals, a couple, met me outside. They'd been delayed crossing the Peace Bridge near Niagara Falls. I recognized them from years before in the Meeting and they recognized me. "There's a real finality in saying goodbye to your Mom, isn't there?" the man asked. I agreed, and soon after walked down the sidewalk; it was a beautiful day. Almost immediately, I thought, "what a weird comment! I mean, this guy is a believer like my mother, so where's the finality he is talking about, when heaven is just a heart attack away, and then, wham, there's my mom, waving at you as you fly on in?"

We had a nice lunch after the service, with lots of small talk, complimentary remarks about my mom and her hospitality, and expressions of how much better off she was now. I mostly listened.

Harvey V., a long-time Meeting friend of my father's, congratulated me on having left the funeral service. I responded that I could remember her much better by myself, than some religious figure I'd never met. I mean, what the hell did he know of my Mom? Had he ridden in the back seat of the car while she drove to and from the grocery store countless times during his life? Had she taken him to Fowler's department store in Binghamton, New York to watch a troupe of Chimpanzees roller skate around in a circle for our amusement? Had he visited The Cider Mill in Endicott, for apple cider and donuts with her? Had he experienced her wistfulness for farm life when we visited the house near Leamington where she was born and raised? No! But I had those memories of my mom, and I wasn't going to allow him to despoil them with religious syrup.

The burial was the next day in southern Ontario. She was returning home, passing through customs and border control for the last time. I don't think she knew where she was going to be buried, but I think it was the right move on my father's part for her to be buried in the country she loved, and in which she grew up, in a spot roughly twenty feet from her sister.

During the graveside ceremony, literally as the casket that held my mother's remains was being lowered into the grave, a life-long friend of hers approached me and said, "Dan, I've heard you have doubts about religion and your salvation. I have a book that I'd like to recommend to you." – Mr. Walker must have possessed a Master's degree in saying the wrong thing at the wrong time. Astonished at his lack of perception regarding the timing of his approach, I turned, faced him and asked, "do you have any doubts about your salvation?" "No," he exclaimed "absolutely not!" – "Since you are being dishonest with yourself," I said somewhat dismissively, "you and your book are of no value to me. Please leave me alone while I mourn my mother." He left quickly and I don't recall seeing him after this exchange. But I do remember his look of surprise at my response to his offer.

Returning home to Arizona, I struggled mentally to accept my mother's death and to place it in some sort of context. Her significant levels of pain and suffering from pancreatic cancer did little except reinforce my agnosticism; in practice, my atheism. Her pain and suffering was up front and personal, inflicted by an evil disease on somebody I loved.

About one month after my mother's death, I ate a reasonable portion of psychedelic mushrooms. During the hours that followed, I was able to reach a certain peace related to my mother's death, and to put myself, and her, and our shared ancestors in our respective positions versus the world and the universe. It helped me see the human race, with its pain and suffering, rising and falling, being born and dying – a circle of life in which I played a role. Yes,

I know psychedelic trips are difficult to describe; putting the experience into words is really not possible. How can one describe living in the moment while on mushrooms, with their can't-get-off-the-moving-train stream of consciousness, afterwards, when they aren't in it? But it was a healing experience for me and I value the insights I uncovered and the peace I felt.

A few years later, one of my friends died, also of cancer. She was about forty one years old. We had attended Fort Lewis College together, along with the man who became her husband. They had two kids, then aged five and six. She died on her little girl's seventh birthday.

Some time not long before she died, I visited, and her husband let me into her room at home, and I listened to her talk through the morphine. I rubbed her feet through her socks, sitting at the foot of the bed away from the medical equipment that was monitoring her vitals and keeping her as pain-free as possible. She was in so much pain, with long periods of sleep and a few moments of clarity. She told me how the doctor had said she might have a few years left, perhaps even to watch her kids graduate from high school, but here she was, in incredible pain and dying just one year after she received that message. Toward the end, she renewed her Catholic faith to some extent, and her service was held in a Catholic church. I understood and accepted her renewed faith. It gave her comfort in the face of uncertainty and death. She was buried at the foot of the Rocky Mountains.

I HAVE DRIED roses from both of these women's funerals; petals from those roses are buried with them. Neither of these women were ready to die; they wanted to live. Nobody had the knowledge or capabilities to heal them. Death is a part of life, but it hurts and only memories are left. If there was a god who created life and was omniscient, omnipotent and kind, I would ask her or him or them (the Trinity?) to heal these two women; stop their pain; raise them from the dead. The parsimonious answer? There is no god who can do that, or if there is one, or more, they are either too busy or unwilling, and if unwilling, heartless. For me, better an uncomfortable truth than a comfortable lie.

32

LETTER TO MY FATHER

D ear Dad –

We have a long history, you and me, initially as father and child-son. That interpersonal dynamic changed once I advanced toward adulthood and began to experience the greater world in which we find ourselves. Like everyone else on this planet, we were born and given a name, which we discover as people begin to call us that. As we grow a bit older, we find ourselves in a situation over which we have no control and for which we had no role in planning. But after a number of years, we begin to realize that we do have some control over who we are, how we want to live our lives and what we believe. Clearly not complete control, given the vagaries of life, but some control.

Thus, after all these years of knowing you, I continue to be puzzled by your voluntary assumption of the role of a dogmatically religious Christian that I assume you were encouraged to adopt, first as a boy by your parents, but then also had, as an adult, to self-select. Clearly we share a similar history, although you are one rung up the ladder from me on a nearly infinite generational ladder. We grew up in households run primarily by adamantly religious fathers. For you, it was Harold; for me, it was you.

We are all born agnostics. Perhaps I could get you to agree to that? Perhaps not. – When we are born, we are ignorant of the world. We do not and cannot know the unknowable. We eat, smile, cry, poop and sleep. But as we grow, first as children and then as adolescents, we begin to witness the world beyond our immediate households which have, if we are fortunate, competent, reputable adults. These adults are, in their very essence, supremely important to our development and learning about the world. We tend to believe what our parents believe and what they teach us, at least until we perceive they aren't completely honest with us. If we discover dishonesty among these respected adults, we may at first assess how deep and wide the dishonesty is, and may subsequently begin to search for alternative sources of knowledge.

So, my puzzle is this: when and how did you discard the agnosticism into which you were born, and how did it come about? Perhaps this question is on the obverse of the same coin upon which is a written question: when did you become "saved"? But I also want to ask, did you not ever have any doubts? Was it the near-fatal car accident you had when you were dating Mom? Was it the pain and suffering you witnessed while serving as a conscientious objector in the medical tents of the Korean War? Something else? Do you have any doubts now in terms of your religious convictions, even if you won't admit them to anyone but yourself? My primary premise is that if you don't admit to having any doubts, or if you staunchly deny or denied those doubts as, say, sinful and thus out of bounds for consideration, you were and are being dishonest with yourself. You were declaring knowledge of the unknowable. So, when and how did you arrive at such a state?

An underlying hypothesis driving these questions is this: You did have doubts about the veracity of your religious beliefs. So, if you had or have doubts, and I would forcefully argue that you did, even if you weren't fully conscious of them, why could you not admit them? More specifically, when you did have doubts, why could you not admit them to yourself and your wife and your kids? Can you not see how such an honest self-assessment and admission would have fundamentally changed the very nature of our family dynamic? Can you not see how it would have made you a more tolerant person?

Looking back at my childhood interactions with you in our roles as son-father, how and why could you not be honest with yourself as a born agnostic, then a strong believer, and not acknowledge the significant belief-threshold over which you had stepped? One day an agnostic, acknowledging you could not truly know whether what you were soon to believe was true or not, and the next day an adamant believer who denied the agnosticism into which you had been born? One day living in the realm of metaphysical gambler who had all his chips in the agnostic square, the next day moving all your chips to the square marked "Biblical God." Was this a step you took based on fear of your own mortality? Was it because of injustice you perceived in the world? What was the catalyst?

Further, assuming that your faith became stronger with time, could you not feel yourself becoming more adamant, more stubbornly entrenched, more dogmatically embedded in your adopted religious belief? If so, or if not, are you not intellectually capable of assessing the effects of this transition on the essence of your character? – Bud wrote about people whose character is deformed by religion; I think you are a perfect example of such a phenomenon. So, also, was your father Harold. Adamant belief feeds dogmatic arrogance and zealotry. Soon afterward, you are judging other people and controlling your children's lives in ways that can only lead to bitterness and rancor. What emotional needs were met by your belief? Was it, is it, fair to trade your personal fear of death for a lifetime of delusion, unsubstantiated promises of heaven, and familial misery?

In a 1989 letter to you, Bud wrote: "The apparent paradox of rigidity and intolerance on the part of people who claim access to ultimate truths is readily resolved by brief reflection. When you think you have all the answers, it is natural that you try to force, to inflict them on others. So you have the phenomenon of major familial unhappiness and despair in almost direct proportion to the piety index. For me, it's not the piety which is primarily objectionable, but rather the arrogance of the attitude behind it, which makes it not only possible but necessary to condemn those who see it otherwise."

To not allow oneself to doubt is to embrace ignorance. Doubting is a way we as humans learn. For children, sometimes what our referent adults tell us is in alignment with objective facts; other times it is not. As we age toward adulthood, many of us shed our child-like gullibility and our teddy bears and begin to think for ourselves, to question what we've been told; others do not. I think you are in the latter category.

Many scientists have expressed dismay regarding how little the general public knows about science, the scientific process and how to interpret its results. Science is one way we as humans know. If you would like to learn more about science, one book I recommend is Lewis Wolpert's (1992), *The Unnatural Nature of Science*.[1]

Science is self-correcting. Scientists, if honest, will readily admit, even celebrate, when they are proved wrong; that is how knowledge is gained. In contrast, you have evidenced a dismissive attitude toward science, scientists and the products of science. You look down on science because scientists test theories, and if theories are found to be incorrect, they change them. In contrast, your beliefs are unchanging and unchangeable. Unlike your beliefs, the results of science are always and forever incomplete. This is not a defect of the scientific method, it's a strength. Evaluating what we know is a continuous process, accomplished by various scientists over time based on accumulating evidence.

In a column in Newsweek, 21st of January 1980, Isaac Asimov[2] stated:

> "There is a cult of ignorance in the United States, and there always has been. The strain of anti-intellectualism has been a constant thread winding its way through our political and cultural life, nurtured by the false notion that democracy means that 'my ignorance is just as good as your knowledge.'"

For me, anti-intellectualism is personified in people like you. I see religious people daily take stances they cannot justify beyond their claim that "this is what I believe; you need to respect my beliefs." My response? No, I don't. There is no equivalence between your beliefs, as you like them, and facts. There are no alternative facts, only unsubstantiated claims, wishful thinking, and lies. I respect your right to believe whatever you want, but I don't have to respect those beliefs. In fact, I don't. I think they do you harm. They certainly have harmed our familial relationships.

In a letter where you finally addressed my letter that used quotes from the Bible to show the murderous side of your god, you said "you reference Jehovah as a slaughterer, and place him along contemporary rulers." You then quoted a verse: "What shall we say then? Is there unrighteousness with God? God forbid" (Romans 9:14, KJV). What a tautology! Next, you said, "I, as you, am a creature. I am not God's defense attorney." And that was that. – In response, I say, "speak for yourself. You unapologetically worship a murderous god. In my view, that makes you an immoral person. It also appears to make you intolerant and judgmental towards other people who live differently and think differently than you do."

In a letter to your four children you once apologized for "being a disciplinarian." To me, your apology was woefully inadequate. Nearly all the pain and suffering inflicted upon our family, primarily by you, could have been avoided if you had simply said, first to yourself, and then to us: "this is what I believe, but I might be wrong." Unfortunately, as I see it, such a moment of self-reflection and self-honesty would represent, for you, a loss of faith. Your will to believe is negatively correlated with intellectual honesty. I assume you would quote a verse, something like: "without faith, it is impossible to please Him," i.e., God (Hebrews 11:6, KJV). But can you not see the logical corner into which you've backed yourself? And can you not understand how your adamant belief negatively affects other people, and especially in the context of this letter, your children?

In a copy of a letter I found in Bud's belongings after he died, written in 1966 from him to you, he wrote: "I close with the plea that you ... study tolerance as an assignment to keep you from the effects of your religion, which is, as you will no doubt admit, essentially an intolerant one." – Clearly, Dad, you never took up that assignment. Otherwise, I think you would have treated your children much better than you did and do; first as children, then as adults. In my assessment, your decision to disregard Bud's plea has not served you, or the family, well. With love, pity and little respect for your adamant beliefs, Dan

---

LETTER TO BUD

D ear Bud –

   I am writing this letter to you as a modern day Rip Van Winkle, not in terms of you having a similar character as Rip, but with me assuming you have awoke from a twenty-five year nap. Clearly, this is wishful thinking on my part. Now in 2025, twenty-five years and more after your death, I continue to miss your love, friendship, and intellectual challenges.

If you were to awaken after twenty five years, you wouldn't be surprised that much has changed. Technology and science continue to push back the frontiers of ignorance, but many people don't pay attention, choosing instead to be comfortable with their own carefully cultivated ignorance. The internet, compared to its relative infancy of twenty-five years ago, is now a wonderful source of knowledge and communication, but despairingly, also a source of conspiracy theories, lies and misinformation. But the world is undeniably more interconnected.

During the past twenty five years, the USA has initiated two major wars, Iraq and Afghanistan, both unilaterally, and at the expense of over 1,000,000 lives, immense pain and suffering, and trillions of dollars – both started by a politician who said he received messages from God. We've also been involved, directly or indirectly, in violent conflicts in Ukraine, Yemen, Pakistan, Libya, Syria, Israel and Palestine. We've had a president, whose qualifications appear to include reality tv "actor," abuser of women, being a racist, and having a history of failed business efforts. Despite all this, he has strong support among many conservative Christians. To them, facts and morality seem not to matter since he gives voice to their fears, biases and prejudices.

Global climate change, which we were aware of in the 1970s, is negatively affecting the lives of a significant portion of the world's population, primarily the poor. In 2020 and 2021, we experienced a world-wide pandemic, with millions of people dead – over one million in the USA alone – partly because of people's lack of belief in the products of science, i.e., namely vaccines. My father, your brother, refused to accept the vaccines, trusting his god, and seems to have gotten away with it.

Clearly, your letters, as written gifts, affected me deeply and continue to do so. With this book, I hope a few more people will also benefit and, as a result, care more about truth and objective reality. – For years, I've thought religion was retreating in the USA, and it is by some counts, at least in the absolute number of religious adherents. This fact isn't, in and of itself, necessarily good or bad, given that religion can be a source of comfort to some people.

But while the absolute number of religious adherents has gotten smaller, those who remain appear to be more fanatical, and think that what is good for them will be, even if forced via the passing of laws, good for the rest of the world. These laws constrain the rights of LGBTQ+ people, women, women to make their personal health decisions, children, immigrants, and others. Many religious fanatics argue in favor of a Christian Theocracy. My father, your brother, asserts that a kingdom is the best form of government and believes Jesus is the best candidate for that role. Welcome to the USA, please set your clocks back 200 years. – Personally, I prefer the rule of law as king, with nobody above it. For me, now as agnostic (technically) and atheist, in practice, I believe society should not tolerate these adamant intrusions into public life. How can you turn the other cheek when somebody is attempting to rip your face off?

For me, a primary takeaway from all this discourse and life-experience is that facts are facts. Denying otherwise leads to a life-time of delusions. My father previously asked us: "where is your hope?" – It's a strange, even hypocritical question given what his hope means for non-believers, i.e., hell. But Thich Nhat Hanh addressed this question meaningfully in his book *Peace is Every Step*.[1] He argued that while hoping things will get better can make the present moment easier to bear, it also takes us away from living in the moment. He argues that "hope [then] becomes a kind of obstacle" to happiness (p. 41). Hope takes us away from working to improve our circumstances now, not only for us but for other people.

In one of your letters to me, you wrote:

> "You say you like to have a God to whom you can confess weaknesses, malfeasances even, someone with whom you can cultivate an essentially 'chummy' relationship. – I think this is one of the most profound of human desires, shared by everyone whose feelings are sensitive enough to be worthy of consideration."

You were right; that's how I felt at the time. However, believing as such means giving up one's intellectual and moral integrity. In hindsight, I see that the Christian's god is unworthy of worship. Other gods appear to be no better.

Clearly, there are reasons fundamentalists believe as they do. Fear of death. A belief that justice will ultimately be served by their god. A salve and balm to push back the pain and suffering of life. However, in another letter, you said, "in all of earth or heaven there is no force, instance, authority or source which can bring home a new fact or interpretation not in harmony with his preconceptions to a fanatical person." Can we, should we, feel compassion for fanatics and fundamentalists? Yes, absolutely. Pity? Yes.

However, when the beliefs of a religious person manifest themselves in the form of persecution, for example, against people who identify as LGBTQ+, we must push back. If a person's adamant religious beliefs incite in their brain hate or bigotry against people with differing sexual preferences or gender identities, various colors of skin, or if they intrude into women's personal healthcare decisions without concern for the obvious complexities, then their religion has corrupted their thinking. I respect their right to believe as they choose, but I don't respect the products of their faith if they are exclusionary, hateful and seek to deprive other people of their constitutional rights, their rights to pursue life, liberty and happiness. They are not entitled to special treatment or deference because of their faith. We cannot allow them to break down the separation of church and state. Their religious freedom must end where our bodies begin.

My father and his fundamentalist-friends believe they are "here on this earth" for a few years, and then go to a place where sorrow and suffering are absent and the streets are paved with gold. I don't know how this lack of sorrow works, because people in heaven will certainly know of somebody who didn't make it, i.e., who was sent to hell. How can they not feel sorrow about that? Will it not be a continuing source of sorrow while they are enjoying endless beers while playing Pinochle with Jesus?

YOU ONCE CLOSED a letter to my father with a plea: "please stay human." In writing this book I suppose I am asserting my role as a social critic. In doing so, I'd ask how we should treat religious fanatics who would force their beliefs on others? This question reminds me of a quote from Henry Wadsworth Longfellow:[2]

> "If we could read the secret history of our enemies, we should find in each person's life, sorrow and suffering to remove all hostility."

As long as religious fanatics keep their beliefs to themselves, I say leave them alone. If, instead, they seek to discriminate and deny equality to all, they must be challenged. They must be stopped.

To them, I would quote from their Bible: "And why beholdest thou the mote that is in thy brother's eye, but considerest not the beam that is in thine own eye?" (Matthew 7, verses 1 and 3, KJV). Further: "Stop imposing pain and suffering on other people based on your emotional wishes, your fervent hopes, your faith, your fantasies."

AS I LOOK BACK on all our correspondence, I so appreciate your patience, empathy, clear analysis, gentle prodding, and your encouragement to think critically about the essential character of the god we once worshipped. Doing so enabled me to see that worshipping a violent god deforms the character of the worshipper. I'm also reminded of Bertrand Russell's (1991) quote you once showed me from his book, *Sceptical Essays*:[3]

> "I wish to propose for the reader's favourable consideration, a doctrine which may, I fear, appear wildly paradoxical and subversive. The doctrine in question is this: that it is undesirable to believe a proposition when there is no ground whatever for supposing it true." He continues, "I must, of course, admit that if such an opinion became common it would completely transform our social life and our political system.... I am also aware (what is more serious) that it would tend to diminish the incomes of clairvoyants, bookmakers, bishops and others who live on the irrational hopes of those who have done nothing to deserve good fortune here or hereafter."

I think these words manifest an essential prescription for our society as it is today.

Moreover, as Richard Dawkins wrote back in 1995, when I agreed with him to a greater extent than I do today, "the universe may be a cold and empty place, with no fairies and no Santa Claus ... and no angels, guardian or garden variety." "But," he continued, "there are also no devils, no hellfire, no wicked witches, no ghosts." And, "there are warm, live, speaking, thinking adult bedfellows to love, and many people find it a more rewarding kind of love than the childish love of stuffed toys."[4] And, I would add, there are loving, non-judgmental family members and mentors like you!

Thus, as I come to the end of this book, I am grateful for your tutelage, your intellectual challenges, for our times of laughter, food, wine, lively conversations, familial love and for our discourse and exchanges of letters – especially yours with your herky-jerky hand-writing. I only wish those times had lasted longer. Love, Dan

AFTERWORD

My father died in early 2025; 93 years old. We didn't talk much in the last few months. When we did, he wasn't mentally clear about life's details, but was quick with biblical references and quotes. I suppose for his sake, I hope his beliefs worked out well for him in the after-life. I doubt I'll ever know.

BIBLIOGRAPHY

Preface

1. Abbey, Edward. *One Life at a Time, Please.* Henry Holt and Company, N.Y., 1988.
2. *A Few Hymns and Some Spiritual Songs, Selected 1856, For the Little Flock,* Oak Park: Bible Truth Publishers.
3. *Echoes of Grace Hymn Book.* Addison, Bible Truth Publishers, 1979.

Chapter 3 - Growing Up In "The Meeting"

1. *A Few Hymns and Some Spiritual Songs, Selected 1856, For the Little Flock,* Oak Park: Bible Truth Publishers.
2. Ice, T., 2010. "John Nelson Darby and the Rapture." *The Journal of Ministry and Theology, 17,* pp.99-119.

Chapter 4 - Meeting Rituals, Teachings and Failures

1. Bunyan, John. *The Pilgrim's Progress.* Grosset and Dunlap.
2. Emerson, Michael O., and David Hartman. "The rise of religious fundamentalism." *Annu. Rev. Sociol.* 32.1 (2006): pp. 127-144.
3. Dawkins, Richard. "Putting Away Childish Things." *Skeptical Inquirer*, vol. 19, no. 1, 1995, pp. 31-36.
4. *Echoes of Grace Hymn Book.* Addison, Bible Truth Publishers, 1979.
5. *A Few Hymns and Some Spiritual Songs, Selected 1856, For the Little Flock,* Oak Park: Bible Truth Publishers.

Chapter 7 - On My Own

1. Gosse, Edmund. *Father and Son.* Penguin Books, London. 1907; 1986, p. 241.

Chapter 9 - On Belief

1. James, William. *Essays in Pragmatism.* Hafner Publishing Co, N.Y., 1948.
2. Smith, Homer. *Man and his Gods.* Little, Brown and Company, N.Y., 1957.

Chapter 10 - Gods and Human Suffering

1. Fowles, John. *The Aristos.* Little, Brown and Company, Boston, 1970.
2. Arouet de Voltaire, Francois-Marie. *Candide or Optimism.* Appleton-Century-Crofts, Inc., N.Y., 1946.

Chapter 12 - Science, Truth And Faith

1. Fowles, John. *The Aristos.* Little, Brown and Company, Boston, 1970.

Chapter 16 - Sincerity, Science And Magic

1. Bunyan, John. *The Pilgrim's Progress.* Grosset and Dunlap.

Chapter 18 - My Conversion

1. Gleick, James. *Genius*, Vintage Books, N.Y., 1992.

Chapter 20 - Bud's Response To My Depressive Feelings

1. Monod, Jacques. *Chance and Necessity.* Fontana, William Collins Sons & Co., Ltd. 1974.

Chapter 32 - Letter To My Father

1. Wolpert, Lewis. *The Unnatural Nature of Science.* Faber and Faber Limited, London, 1992.
2. Asimov, Isaac. "A Cult of Ignorance (My Turn)," January 21, *Newsweek*, p. 19, 1980.

Chapter 33 - Letter To Bud

1. Hanh, Thich Nhat. *Peace is Every Step: The Path of Mindfulness in Everyday Life.* Bantam, N.Y., 1992.
2. Longfellow, Henry Wadsworth. *The Complete Works of Henry Wadsworth Longfellow: The Golden Legend*, HardPress, 2018.
3. Russell, Bertrand. *Sceptical Essays*, Routledge, N.Y., 1991.
4. Dawkins, Richard. "Putting Away Childish Things." *Skeptical Inquirer*, vol. 19, no. 1, 1995, p. 36.

ABOUT THE AUTHOR

Daniel R. Krause grew up in a fundamentalist Christian household in the eastern USA in the 1960s and 70s. In his early twenties, he moved west, first to Colorado where he attended Fort Lewis College, and next to Arizona, where he attended Arizona State University. He enjoys international travel, bicycling, hiking and lives happily with his wife and their two Labrador Retrievers.

He receives email at drk.truthandfear@proton.me